BREAD AND ROSES

Nontheism and the Human Spirit

Muriel Seltman

Matador
9 Priory Business Park
Kibworth Beauchamp
Leicestershire LE8 0RX, UK
Tel: (+44) 116 279 2299
Fax: (+44) 116 279 2277
Email: books@troubador.co.uk
Web: www.troubador.co.uk/matador

ISBN 978 1780884 912

British Library Cataloguing in Publication Data.
A catalogue record for this book is available from the British Library.

Printed and bound in the UK by TJ International, Padstow, Cornwall
Typeset in 11pt Book Antiqua by Troubador Publishing Ltd, Leicester, UK

Matador is an imprint of Troubador Publishing Ltd

For my sister Ruth Goldsmith whose encouragement and understanding have been invaluable. Thank you, Ruth.

Contents

Prologue

This is not an academic work and it certainly has no pretensions to academic rigour. It is a cross between a series of essays and an indication of my own spiritual journey. It is a combination of the discursive and the personal and begins around 2002 when I was 75 and became an Attender at a Quaker Meeting, although I had realised for many years previously that I had a spiritual (that is to say non-material) dimension to my life. I hasten to emphasise that the word 'spiritual' is used here and throughout in the same sense in which it is used when referring to the 'human spirit'. Even more than this, it means that aspect of the human spirit which is most positive, that which is said to make us human in the fullest and best sense.

This followed on many decades in which politics were paramount for me and was really a follow-on to this past life, which I have never jettisoned. I would still call myself a Marxist-Humanist-Nontheist-Quaker.

Why, then, go to the trouble and anguish of embarking on this book at the age of 84?

First, I would like to rescue nontheism (or atheism as it is more commonly called) from the negative press it has had from theists for a long time and in the last few years in particular. Nontheist writers have been accused of bigotry, rigidity and ignorance of the case for the existence of God; that is, a transcendental deity who created and in some sense, rules the universe.

This is an attempt by a lay person in the field to present nontheism as it is for me, and might in a general sense be for other people, and not as it is often thought to be. My own experience is that nontheism is a living, open process in which lack of restriction to a particular doctrine or scripture has freed me to realise my true self, including the ability to appreciate more deeply than ever before the implications of the insights of theism itself. It was amazing to find myself with a new understanding of the very belief system which I had jettisoned so many years before. And this is because it has been possible to stand back and view it from another dimension, without intellectual or emotional shackles.

It is lovely to think and feel with a minimum tie to one's past. There are few more exciting mental experiences than reflecting upon the concepts of 'life, death, the universe and everything' with maximum freedom and starting with as few presuppositions as possible. Even in old age it is possible to become excited by the sheer unexpectedness of where one's thoughts lead.

I cannot now believe that for a large part of my life I did not recognise my spiritual dimension. This recognition occurred about 30 years ago. I then found myself embarked upon a spiritual journey, not with deliberate intention but as an automatic reaction to my life as it had been and was.

Previous to that, from being a teenager onwards, my life and thoughts had been dominated by political thought and action. It did not enter my head until recently that my political ideas and yearnings were part of my life's spiritual journey. I would have vigorously denied this and would have seen myself as a material being whose thoughts, emotions and so forth were a function of my materiality.

From my early teenage years I had a passion for mathematics and the implications of 'modern' physics (Relativity and Quantum Theory) that I read about in *The Evolution of Physics* by Albert Einstein and Leopold Infeld. It was so captivating that, although I did not really understand it and although my natural ability was in history, I began to work extremely hard at mathematics and science because I could not bear the thought of being cut off from them after leaving school. I knew that if I worked hard enough and long enough I would understand this particular book. I graduated in mathematics, later studied the history of science and the history of mathematics and have had a passionate love affair with these to this very day.

Again, it was only in recent years that I recognised that my emotions in relation to mathematics and what might be termed the 'Quantum World' were and are an essential part of my life of the spirit. They were a powerful factor in causing me to become a nontheist in the smoothest and easiest way imaginable.

Throughout my life they have provided a basis for my thinking and an inexhaustible source of spiritual joy. Mathematics achieved this through its connection with the embedded, potentially mathematical features of the natural world and through its sheer beauty. Science achieved this through the miracle of its methodology and the fact that this methodology reveals the contingent, unpredictable, indeterminate, acausal reality that lies beneath the stability and continuity of what we experience at our own level.

For the last several years, I have felt myself coming together into a seamless whole and it has felt very good indeed. More than merely coming together, all aspects of my spiritual dimension interpenetrate. My 'self' is no longer fractured. I can no longer distinguish the struggle for a better world from my spiritual journey, which includes my love of mathematics and science. They all enhance each other. Not only that, each is an essential prerequisite for the other. It must be obvious that to concentrate on one's own spiritual journey to the exclusion of the world one lives in and the needs of other people is selfish in the extreme. Equally, to expect to have a revolution in society which is at all meaningful, and which is not merely a change of personnel but retains the same old hierarchies and power-structures under another name, without a transfiguration of hearts and minds, would at best be a waste of everybody's time and at worst may be a disaster.

In case there is any confusion on this point, it must be stressed that religious institutions should always be distinguished from the essence of the belief systems which such institutions embody and from the individual people who seek their source of meaning and ultimate happiness in such religions. Religious institutions have consistently played a major role in the maintenance of social control. They achieved this by 'hijacking' the spiritual dimension and exploiting the yearnings of oppressed humanity. Moreover, monstrous crimes have been committed in the name of religion by religious authorities.

Finally, it seems to me important to convey to as many other people as possible the depths of the spiritual joy that nontheists experience (just as theists do) from music, poetry, dance and other arts, nature, friendship and love. The joy is equally great for theists and nontheists alike even though we nontheists do not place the origin of such phenomena and the resulting joy outside the universe. We see the universe as perfectly capable of creating all of this for itself.

However, I do know that it would be wrong and one-sided to see the situation through rose-tinted spectacles. We all need comforting at many times in our lives and such comfort is easily obtainable from a fatherly but all-powerful figure in the sky accompanied by lovely heart-warming myths such as the Christmas story. Are we willing to sacrifice such comfort for the challenging but scary independence and freedom of thought which is the reward for standing on one's own intellectual and spiritual feet?

Moreover, we all have a deep-seated yearning for meaning and religions may provide this. Nothing is more important than questions such as: Why am I here? What is my relation to the universe? How is it possible that I am here at all? Where was I before I was born? And over and above these: where shall I go after I am dead? It is a commonplace even to mention such questions which are so universal as to provide a link between all of humanity. Do we have to do without meaning if we relinquish a creator-father figure?

I think that there are satisfactory answers to these problems and I hope to point to at least some of these in the course of this book although I have absolutely no intention of proselytising. It is, however, my heartfelt wish that this work will help some people to see things differently and thus lessen, at least fractionally, the weight of oppression that bends the backs of millions who are made to see themselves as helpless in the face of an all-powerful divinity who inflicts barbaric punishments for eternity upon those who do not obey his rules and regulations. This is the link between my political and spiritual selves.

We have to reclaim our own human spirit and a massive rescue operation is called for. Such a rescue operation is a vital part of the liberation of humankind. It is not separate from the drive towards a better world in the social/political sphere but is a major part of it. No new political and economic system can have a hope of flourishing or even being struggled for without a major change of hearts and minds.

This is the reason for the title of this book. It is a tribute to the women strikers at a textile mill in Massachusetts in 1912 who had a banner which read: 'Give us bread, but give us roses.'

Introduction

The first mention of God I can remember occurred when I had just turned six. My mother had very recently died and I liked to get into bed with my father, obviously for some sort of comfort. After I had done this a few times he must have begun to feel uncomfortable about it because there came the occasion when he pushed me away and out of the bed with the words, "God doesn't like little girls to sleep with their daddies after they're six." As I recall it, my response was total acceptance without query. However, it is worthwhile to explore briefly the logic of what he said, however well meant it was.

a) God, in all his omnipotence was presupposed;

b) God has likes and dislikes of an arbitrary, unexplained character;

c)There were sexual implications that I was unaware of at the time.

Many children must have experienced similar conditioning. Is it any wonder, then, that for so many people these ideas are so firmly rooted that logic alone is insufficient to overcome their effect in later life? For this reason, it is necessary to dispense with the idea that a person is necessarily either a believer in God or a nonbeliever, a theist or nontheist. People just do not work like that. A human being is never a total, monolithic whole. Life is messier than that and each of us is a mixture of reason and emotion, likes and dislikes, certainties and doubts, and each of these is predominant under differing circumstances.

This is not to say that there are not people who are certain which side they are on with respect to any particular issue and who remain fairly consistent in the face of the contingencies which present themselves in the course of life. I think we must face the fact that there are a considerable number of people who are permanently in a state of tension between belief and nonbelief. Many others simply put the problem to one side.

This book has those people especially in mind. It is about nontheism but does not repeat all the arguments for and against a transcendental deity, which have already been very ably put by highly-qualified and well-informed writers. Rather, it sets out to reflect upon those arguments, especially in Chapter 3.

What I would like to convey to the reader in what is to come is, firstly, the spiritual joy that is attainable without presupposing a creator God. Secondly, I would hope that some readers at least would gain some idea of the autonomy and spiritual freedom attainable by jettisoning the cumbersome conditioning of childhood. Freedom may be very scary but it is worthwhile feeling a little scared at first in order to end up having freedom of thought and intellectual autonomy. Even though it is tempting to cling to a spiritual prison because it provides you with a roof over your head, food and a form of security, the door is actually wide open and you can walk out whenever you want.

My own journey was slightly unusual. I was nearly 60 when I realised that I and everybody around me has a spiritual dimension. The human spirit is manifested all around us in a variety of ways. We can see it in everybody we meet. We experience it ourselves every time we listen to music which transfigures us. Or it may be that what 'turns on' our spirit is poetry or dance or something else.

There is a strange idea abroad that nontheists think that human beings have only a physical side, that all that exists is the material world. Why should this have to be the case? We all experience mental and spiritual phenomena all the time. If we were exclusively material, how could we account for our ideas, emotions, attitudes and that these change? How could we account for the fact that we have sudden unexpected insights and changes in our beliefs?

At the time when I would have called myself a materialist, I would have quoted Frederick Engels (Karl Marx's great collaborator) who said that we should see the world exactly as it is without any transcendental admixture. Well, I still do see the world like this. But there is nothing transcendental in anything that is part of the universe we live in. Ideas (mental phenomena) and the spiritual emotions evoked by music are certainly part of the world we live in – we experience them. They are part of the universe. Therefore they are not transcendental.

There are those who might say that the music of Bach was inspired from outside, i.e. by God. My reply to this would be that this is a supposition only and, furthermore, that the universe is perfectly capable of creating the St Matthew Passion. Do not forget that Johann Sebastian Bach was, himself, an integral part of the universe.

Every human being has, of necessity, a form of spiritual life however distorted it may be or however limited or undeveloped it remains. This is so because our total consciousness is an emergent property of our physical selves, suitably organised. The sad thing is that so many people lead unfulfilled spiritual lives on account of the constraints exerted on them by their conditioning.

I would hope that this little book might assist some readers, even in a small way, to have a renewed spiritual life which transcends anything they have experienced before. But the words written below could never accomplish this gigantic feat. This is a small piece of writing. It can only point to possibilities by calling on the experience of one ordinary individual. Its primary function is to open the eyes of readers to possibilities which they may explore and develop for themselves. This is surely more fun than merely accepting a system of religion which they had no part in constructing for themselves.

For most people, even those in so-called advanced countries, life can be hard, so hard that it seems as if the only thing that makes it bearable is a comforting and authoritative God who had created us all and with whom every single one of us has a personal relationship. However, if such a creator were to exist I cannot see that this would give him the right to dictate how we lead our individual lives right down to the details of what we eat or drink, how we (women) dress or when and with whom we perform acts of bodily love. It would certainly not give him the right to dictate what we think. Such a creator would have no more right to dictate our ethics or morals than a parent has the right to dictate the thoughts, morals and ethics of grown-up children. And it certainly would not follow that because a set of stories about our ancestors and their alleged connection with such a God was written poetically and had a beauty of its own, that these must be accepted as absolute truth, relevant for all time and not subject to reinterpretation and reassessment.

The idea for this book took shape as I watched people I knew grappling with the problems of belief and searching for meaning in their lives. These are educated, thinking people who read widely but cannot go along with the arguments for nontheism, not because they find them unacceptable but because nontheism often sounds comfortless and would deprive their lives of meaning. 'There must be something out there. Else why are we here at all?' And the 'good fortune' argument may rear its head: Something happened, perhaps they were very ill, close to death and were apparently miraculously saved after praying, as a last resort. Although such a conclusion is understandable it is definitely not logical. Moreover, and far worse than going along with a *post hoc, ergo propter hoc* inference, it presents a God who has chosen to answer their particular prayers in preference to all the millions to whom he has not chosen to extend a helping hand. In the end, it became a pressing need to express my own views in the light of my own experience, in the hope that this extra perspective might help others along their own road.

Chapters 1, 2 and 3 are based upon my own spiritual journey since the time when I realised I had a spiritual dimension and later became a Quaker. It must be stressed that 'spirit' and 'spiritual' are used in this book as they would be understood in the phrase 'human spirit'. Normally, people hearing the word 'spiritual' assume that this means something religious and such an assumption is understandable. However, throughout what follows, neither 'spirit' nor 'spiritual' has a religious implication but refers to a non-material, conscious aspect of humanity. Chapter 1 discusses Quaker beliefs and practices and indicates how these fit well into my nontheist framework. Chapter 2 raises the possibility of a self-referring universe and, after explaining what is meant by this, suggests some implications for nontheists, especially our relationship to the cosmos and our search for meaning. Chapter 3 continues with some reflections upon some of the issues connected with the existence and nature of God. Chapters 1, 2 and 3 are roughly chronological. They are a logical reconstruction of my spiritual journey and thoughts over the last ten years or so and are laid out under different headings for the sake of coherence.

Chapters 4 and 5 focus on mathematics and physics. At first sight they might appear to stand out from the rest of the book to the point of being intrusive. They are, however, as has been fully explained in the Prologue, an integral part of my own adventures of the spirit and an indispensable part of my reasons for being a nontheist.

This is particularly the case with respect to mathematics. I can only explain this by comparing the transformative aesthetic appreciation of mathematics with the same feelings engendered by music. Many readers will understand this immediately. Of course, the experiences are different but they are of the same quality and other mathematicians will know precisely what I mean. You only have to see the eyes of many mathematicians light up as they talk about the aspects of the field which transports them to see the truth of this.

It is slightly different in the case of science. Transformative emotions are aroused in me by what is called 'modern' physics, particularly Quantum Mechanics because it reveals a totally unexpected world at the subatomic level in which the apparently 'normal' rules of the experiential level are routinely broken. In place of the staid, deterministic, cause-and-effect ruled familiar scenario, scientific reasoning and experiment have brought to light the uncertain, unpredictable, contingent aspect of the physical universe. These two chapters were left until after the first three (even though they should be first chronologically) in case potential readers might be frightened off by the very words 'mathematics and physics'.

Here I must offer some reassurance to the timid reader. Certainly, there are some technicalities which might be unfamiliar and, perhaps, daunting. Rest assured, however, that much care has been taken to render them understandable and to make everything as clear as possible. I hope they will be accessible to the reader who is prepared to read slowly (sometimes) or even to read some paragraphs twice.

Mathematics and certain branches of physics have given me so much in my life that I could not bear to leave them out. They were what 'turned me on' as a youngster and impelled me to study them further. This is why they were chosen. Many readers will be familiar with many of the ideas already and some will be far more knowledgeable than I am, so they do not need any warning about difficulty. It is the others whom I am concerned about and hope to interest.

Chapter 6, 'Gathering the Threads Together' attempts to do precisely this but does stray into further implications such as the section on 'Self-Transformation'. The 'Personal Finale' expresses my gratitude to nature that we do not know when we are going to die. At the age of 85, I still have spiritual insights and, although I know that it is not the case, I feel that the time ahead of me in which to have more of these insights is limitless.

CHAPTER 1

Quakers and the Human Spirit

It was when I was 75 and had recognised a spiritual dimension for some time, that I felt rather low and in need of what I termed 'spiritual support'. I had had a brief contact with Dublin Quakers when I was a young student and I decided that a Quaker Meeting might give me the spiritual support I needed now. Having found the address of my nearest Meeting, I duly went along the following Sunday morning and, like many other people I now know, I sat down in the Meeting Room , in which there were already several other people sitting in silence, and immediately felt completely at home.

Quakerism in General

What is it about Quakers that so 'speaks to my condition' as Quakers say? Especially as I am also a Marxist-Humanist-Nontheist. The first thing that comes to mind is the absence of any specific creed or dogma. Each of us is free to travel our personal spiritual journey without interference. This is the most attractive feature of all as far as I am concerned.

Probably the first thing any Quaker will mention if

asked what he/she believes is that 'there is that of God/Light/Good in everybody'. Such optimism about human nature is a principal distinguishing feature of Quakers. No mention of sin, original or otherwise and a consistent, sometimes irritating way of seeing *only* the best in people and situations. But it is a very positive characteristic. Moreover, Quakers believe in looking inward and not outward to an external authority for the source of meaning in our lives.

Equally positive are the so-called 'testimonies' – principles which Quakers subscribe to and which I am sure I shall never discard even though I may refine my understanding of them: simplicity, truthfulness, integrity, equality, peace and sustainability (of the planet). These testimonies are most important in holding the Society of Friends together.

And in case the principle of looking inward for meaning elicits the accusation of navel-gazing, the other, outward-looking aspect of Quakers has to be remembered – the constant search for a way to repair some damage in the world, to alleviate suffering, to right injustice. I might have labelled this 'reformism' in my earlier days but now I know that one cannot wait for revolution in order to improve things and that the time for action of some sort is here and now.

Quakers say they understand the truth by experience and not through authority. Such experience is not intended to mean only ordinary, everyday experience but also spiritual experience. George Fox (1624 – 1691), the 'father-figure' of the Society of Friends, sometimes uses 'experimental' in place of 'experiential'. This presents no problem because at that time the word 'experimental' did not mean what it means today, that is, an exact scientific method of procedure. This was not formalised until the late seventeenth century and early eighteenth centuries. The two words, 'experiential' and 'experimental' were almost interchangeable at the time that Fox was writing.

Spiritual experience is, by definition, individual. I know what I mean by my own spiritual/intellectual experience but I have no way of comparing it with that of others as there is no objective means of comparison. The closest I can get to describing accurately what I mean is to point to the experience of listening to music which transfigures, which penetrates one's being and elevates one to a higher level, unachievable in the ordinary course of events.

On no occasion have I experienced anything that I could construe as a being outside normal experience, of the sort that religious people would call 'God'. Since Quakers base individual belief on what is called 'experience' and as I have no personal, spiritual experience of a transcendental being, I am left with no basis for such a belief. I am a nontheist Quaker. Experience is both intuitive and rational and I have no experience of anything I would label as 'God'. I accept this as I accept the experience of the holiness of the human spirit which emanates from the people I meet.

Originally, understanding the truth through experience must have meant a rejection of authority, an assertion of the freedom of the individual to decide for himself. However, experience is a potential hazard used as an *exclusive* criterion for truth or falsity. It is arbitrary, based as it is on the individual event(s); it is selective insofar as we inevitably choose what is significant and what is not significant in our lives; it is by no means neutral as it is subject to our own interpretation; and it is determined as much by cultural background and preferences as anything else. Alone, it is not reliable. It is objectively untestable. However, taken together with rationality as Quakers mean, it is decisive.

After all, all experiences are subject to being reflected upon and assessed by the one experiencing them and, therefore, subject to rational/logical investigation. We experience things as a whole person with the inevitable participation of both the intuitive and the rational/logical. When George Fox and the early Quakers spoke of 'experience' or 'experiment' they were stressing the necessity of trusting one's own judgement, of standing on one's own intellectual feet, so to speak. It is simply that experience on its own is not always a good test of the truth of things – Galileo, when writing in defence of the heliocentric solar system, said that we should not always believe simply the evidence of our senses and he was right.

It is sad but true that millions of people hope that praying to God for their loved ones who are very ill or after, say, a bad accident, will cause the almighty to intervene – but surely the omnipotent deity could have prevented the illness in the first place? Or stopped the car crash? And how many starving people all over the world are told and believe that 'God will provide' when he very clearly has not done so and shows no signs of ever doing this? If they took to heart the Quaker injunction of basing their belief on experience, they would not for one minute be taken in. Who knows what changes might be effected and how much better a world we might have?

Many theists speak as if we simply have to sit back and 'experience' God, which prejudges the issue of such a God's existence. Alleged experience of God is usually expressed in terms of normal experience, except that it sounds more intense. A feeling of being surrounded by all-inclusive love? This is described as 'God' which certainly prejudges the issue. Why should such an experience be supposed to 'prove' the existence of a transcendental being when the description is clearly one of a being who participates in our universe? This thoroughly belittles the notion of the potential immanence of a putative God. To be like a loving father is not the same thing as being immanent.

The refreshing thing about Quakers is the affirmation of the possibility of direct contact with what theists would call God or, as I would say, Actuality or Suchness. And so, in Quaker practice, there is no priesthood, no sacraments and no symbols. What a relief. Symbols, statues and clerics can be such a distraction from Actuality and it is peaceful and calming to be without them. The absence of symbols in a stark, undecorated Meeting Room makes a fitting space in which to hold a Meeting in which the participants simply sit and, each in their own way, identify themselves with Reality/Actuality/Suchness, insofar as they are able.

Members of the Meeting do not look outwards for

the ultimate but inwards. The principal founder and organiser of Quakers, George Fox, was especially emphatic about this and in a way which was immensely courageous. People should have the courage to believe in themselves, to accept the evidence of their inward experience. There is no need to look outward towards some other, external authority. We should each of us stand on our own feet and have confidence in ourselves. What an extraordinarily forward-looking and sound piece of advice that was.

Another aspect to Quaker belief is the property it has in common with science – its relativity and provisionality – which emerges from the developmental side. This is a precious aspect of Quaker belief and it links with openness to every aspect of the cosmos, material and non-material. Each individual is seen as travelling a spiritual road, every person at a different point but with no suggestion that anyone is 'more advanced' than anyone else. There is no suggestion of a hierarchy of spiritual 'levels'. Everyone is progressing but every step is a first step and feels like a new beginning.

I must insert here the caveat that I am describing the ideal situation. In practice, Quakers are ordinary people. Each Meeting is a microcosm of society. The difference is that Quaker ideals are aimed at. We are all spiritually equal, however much of a newcomer one is to the Meeting.

Many theist Quakers also have a concept of God which is non-absolute and, in fact, developmental and without the baggage of doctrinal attachments. This is not universal but is the case amongst those whom I know. Unity in diversity and diversity within unity. And openness to ideas of all sorts. What more could one ask for?

Paradoxically, what one might want is more recognition that not all belief systems (secular or religious) are equally acceptable, more recognition of the need for putting boundaries to tolerance where these are required; at least the recognition of difference. Occasionally, Quakers talk as if all belief systems were really the same despite surface appearances to the contrary. However, the truth is that there are unacceptable belief systems based on unacceptable axioms which result in unacceptable practical consequences. Quakers have always been exceptionally strong in opposing racism or colour prejudice but are on less solid ground when it comes to religions. Respect for other people is essential, respect for what is acceptable in their belief system is necessary. But never for what are unacceptable in today's world of respect for human rights and principles of equality. We must never be cultural relativists where this conflicts with such criteria. Our cultural relativity must be limited to what is acceptable in today's world and must never extend to what might have been acceptable hundreds of years ago. There must be a reason why we sit in a Quaker Meeting room and not a synagogue, mosque, temple or church. We have chosen this in preference to the others. We should not see all beliefs as equally valid.

A particularly admirable aspect of Quaker belief and practice is its anti-authoritarian character, deriving directly from 17th century roots. Even Quaker organisation and the proper conduct of Quaker business is non-hierarchical. In his marvellous book, *The Trouble with God,* David Boulton suggests that we should replace the notion of the Kingdom of Heaven by the Republic of Heaven. I would extend this idea by saying that the United States is a republic but is far from being truly democratic. There are still the very powerful, the less powerful and those without power. Perhaps we need a Commune of Heaven in which all sit equally and leadership is rotated on the basis of functional necessity. Quakers approach this totally in spirit even if the practice is not always perfect.

In the early period (second half of the seventeenth century), Quakers were opposed to the established Church, which they rightly regarded as corrupt, and many early Quakers went to prison and/or were tortured for refusal to pay tithes and perform the required obeisance to the clergy. There are deeply moving accounts of how the children of early Quakers kept their Meeting going when the grown-ups were all in prison.

What they were suffering for was freedom of belief, freedom of speech – the essence of the individual rights that would go forward to the future and which we in the UK (mostly) enjoy today.

In its Christian form in the seventeenth century, Quaker(ism) was the logical outcome of Protestantism. Today, while still retaining Christian roots but 'open to new light', much in the beliefs of Quakers (in the UK anyway) has transcended its early format and approaches a new spirituality, free of all doctrinaire shackles. It feels good to be amongst people whose spiritual development lies in a DIY spirit. Each stands on her/his own spiritual feet, if one can put it that way, but with the support and boundaries of the collective.

The key words are openness, freedom, provisionality and indeterminacy. Of these, indeterminacy is the most engaging. It derives, not from scepticism or wavering but from the very openness to the cosmos which is the hallmark of being a Quaker. And it may be that the developmental aspect (Becoming) together with the (unchanging) Being of the process of the Quaker belief system necessarily involves a form of uncertainty.

Procedures in a Quaker Meeting

There is nothing quite like a Quaker Meeting. The main characteristic is the silence, which has a calm stillness all its own. The Meeting Room expresses the egalitarian nature of the Society of Friends as the participants normally sit in a circle. It is stark and free of images of any kind, which expresses the unqualified opposition to any form of idolatry. There is no cleric but only participants, which expresses the direct access to whatever exists. There is no need of a mediator between the participants and whatever is in the universe. Everyone is free to speak and all try to 'listen creatively', that is, listen to what the heart or essence of the ministry is, so that there is a proper sympathy with the giver of the ministry and no sense of criticism. This emerged from the revolutionary character of early Quakerism.

When early Quakers refused to have an intermediary between them and their God they took this to its logical conclusion.

When a Quaker is moved to stand up and share the insight which has come from deep inside – give ministry – this is understood to be, not a function of her/his ego, not an urge to press opinions upon others or to demonstrate virtue (like the Pharisee in the Bible) but to share an insight. The words are a gift to the Meeting. The Quaker ministers because it is impossible not to do so. At least this is the ideal.

It sometimes feels sacrilegious to stand up and, literally, 'break' the silence by saying something. And yet it has rightly been said that the spoken words of ministry should 'grow out of' the silence. My experience has been that, however much I try to moderate the sound of my voice, nevertheless the beginning of what I say appears to 'break' into the silence, to disrupt it, to break the continuity of the process of the Meeting. Sometimes, some spoken ministry appears obvious or one disagrees with it. But such ministry is not a debate. Listeners are enjoined to go to the heart of what is said, the essence behind the spoken words so that they are able to empathise with the core of the message.

Finally, how do I react to the use of ideas such as 'worship' or references by some other Quakers to 'God' or 'Christ'? And what about the use of the word 'church' to refer to the Society of Friends? How do I cope with these? Often with a great deal of difficulty. At other times, I can translate them, take them in my stride or even ignore them.

These four words are the ones causing difficulty – Church, worship, God and Christ. Surely we are a Meeting and go to Meeting in a Meeting House? George Fox referred to churches as 'steeple-houses'. We must strictly distinguish institutional Churches from the beliefs held dear by the masses of the population, especially since the first are steeped in guilt for crimes over the centuries – wars and the blessing of wars, massacres and pogroms. 'Worship' is easier to cope with – it means respect, reverence and love. It need not be associated with God but could refer to the universe itself. 'God' is harder. 'God' may be seen as an idea, an abstraction, firstly from all things good, all things beautiful and all things infinite, in fact from all perfection; and then the abstraction from all of these. That is, the word 'God' is an abstraction from abstractions. There are other viewpoints (see below p.150).

'Christ' is definitely extremely hard for me to swallow. This is the Greek for 'saviour' or 'anointed' and is not a sort of surname for a man whose Aramaic name was Yeshua and whose Hebrew name was Joshua. 'Jesus Christ' was ultimately the creation of the Church after they had transformed Yeshua of Nazareth out of all recognition.

One final point in this sort of connection. It is sad but, unfortunately, true that many Jewish people (and I am one of them), view the sign of the cross with fear and horror. This may well be a sort of folk memory of countless pogroms and massacres against Jews undertaken over 2,000 years under the aegis of Christian

Churches of various denominations in the name of 'The Jews killed Christ'. This last, though, has nothing to do with Quakers.

More on Quaker Silence

Most members or attenders, if asked what is their favourite aspect of Quaker life, would say, 'The silence of the Meeting'. Much has already been written about this so that I will simply say that it can be totally magical to walk into a Meeting Room in which participants are already sitting in silence and simply sit down and join them.

Quakers meet together in silence, perhaps waiting to be 'led' (to stand up and speak), perhaps profiting from the sense of support from others. I do not wait for anything but hope just 'to be' as far as possible.

Sometimes, there is the (almost) magical experience of a 'gathered Meeting' when there is a kind of coincidence of calm, when, for the maximum number of participants, the cares and troubles of everyday life (the Becoming aspect of our lives), have slipped away. This silence has a quality all of its own.

I am a nontheist so my experience will not correspond to that of theists who see this as waiting for 'leadings from the Holy Spirit or God'. For me, it is simply a matter of being open to the Suchness of the cosmos. Most importantly, it involves for me '*Being* in the silence'. I begin with the cares of the world fighting for control of my mind and, after a while, if I am fortunate, the Being of my consciousness predominates over the Becoming. (It is obvious that neither aspect can ever totally disappear). So life-giving is this experience that if I miss going to Meeting for one reason or another, I feel 'withdrawal symptoms' and wait impatiently for the following week.

There are many different forms of silence. We can talk of an ominous silence, a dead silence, a pregnant silence, an awkward silence, a shocked silence and there are, no doubt others I have not thought of. None of these is like that of a Quaker Meeting.

Perhaps 'stillness' would be a better word but neither 'stillness' nor 'silence' is fully adequate because a Quaker Meeting is never completely silent or totally still. People fidget, cough, sneeze and babies sometimes add their own engaging sounds. Quaker silence is not the silence of nothingness, of emptiness. We are all united, however, in looking inward and not outward for what we are seeking.

Any Quaker Meeting satisfies two pairs of (apparently) contradictory needs. First, there is the need for solitude and lack of social pressure on one hand and, on the other hand, the need for support from others. The second contradiction is between the joy and peace of a totally silent Meeting and, on the other hand, the fact that this is so only in relation to the need for vocal ministry if it is to be a true Meeting and not just a collection of people sitting in silence in the same room. Such contradictions are endemic to the situation and present no problems and, in a way, they heighten the experience of the Meeting.

It has been said that ministry should be given so as to 'carry the silence' with it. This is not easy because every example of ministry to a small extent 'breaks the silence'. We have to live with this as a fact of life. We go to Meeting to obtain the sense of spiritual support that only the consciousness of others travelling a similar road can give. It would be different to sit in a room at home and simply say nothing.

Silence is a deeply exciting mystery. Associated with the void and emptiness, it nevertheless is usually full of content of all sorts. It is especially mysterious in its identification with nothingness or a void because in thinking of nothingness or a void we always imagine *something* – it is impossible to do anything else.

Despite this, it should be borne in mind that the universe has existed for more than thirteen billion years and for almost the whole of this time there was total silence. Not until sentient beings emerged, possessing the organs whereby the waves travelling through space could be translated into sounds, was there sound. There were no sounds until there were ears (or other equivalent organs) to hear them. The 'Big Bang', if it occurred, must have been absolutely silent. Noise has to be heard. So silence is much more typical than sound – there have been sounds for only a tiny fraction of the time during which the universe has existed.

Further, and closer to home, we are all aware of the significance of the silence (gaps) between words and how much difference it makes when there are gaps of different lengths between phrases or sentences. Such silences are essential to create meaning. The same applies to music (perhaps more so) and when people say 'the timing was perfect' in relation to an actor or comedian, they are referring to the same thing and this is a great compliment.

Finally, another and rather different point about silence, which is, I think, intriguing. Zero is a number with special properties. Added to the right-hand end of any whole number it multiplies it by ten, two zeros multiply it by a hundred and so on. Placed between the two digits 2 and 3 in the number 23, that number becomes 203, a very different number with different properties. Any number raised to the power zero equals 1. Zero added to or subtracted from any number leaves that number unchanged. Any number multiplied by zero equals zero. Thus, the power of zero *in relation to* other numbers is enormous.

Similarly, the power of silence *in relation to* sounds is enormous. Thus, the power of silence *in relation to* sounds resembles (corresponds to) the power of zero *in relation to* other numbers.

Such a correspondence, viewed in this way, brings me an unjustified and childish pleasure, which derives from the coming-together of two cherished aspects of my life. Zero relates ultimately to the *nothingness* that underlies the cosmos viewed abstractly and Quaker silence similarly relates to the *nothingness* of a cosmos stripped of attributes but arrived at from a different starting-point, a very concrete one.

More on Ministry

It is ministry which overtly links the individual with the collective experience. Someone has risen to their feet to share some thoughts which appear to the speaker to be sufficiently important to be put into spoken words.

There must be those who feel relieved when this happens because newcomers might find the silence scary. It is scary in the same way that freedom is scary for those used to noise and bustle all the time. A Quaker Meeting is different from the services conducted by clerics in which there is a lot of sound, hymns, sermons, prayers, chanting and formal statements of belief. To sit in silence for a whole hour puts people on their mettle – there is no external authority and people are thrown on their own resources.

There is, in fact, a deep problem involved in ministry. It has been put like this: 'What you cannot say about God is deeper than what you can say'. This applies to all significant statements, not only references to God. Speech always diminishes thought and the emotion accompanying it. We sometimes forget that words are only symbols, pointers if you like, and as symbols they embody in an expressible form what is inexpressible.

A sort of paradox is inevitable in ministering:

> If I speak, I should not, because the thought is diminished.
> If I do not speak, I should, otherwise the thought will not be communicated.

Some years ago I was at a meeting where a facilitator said that one should not get up and minister if it is an ego trip. This is right, of course, taken simplistically but it is surely the case that the ego is bound to be involved in standing up in front of a number of people and sharing one's thoughts, even if the involvement is the fear of boring them or looking silly. It is not necessarily a question of wanting to show off one's virtue or speaking skills.

The problem does not only lie in such subjective worries, which are the problem only of the person ministering. The problem also exists for the listeners who have the duty of discerning the essence of what is being said, that which comes from the heart.

Quakers and Christianity

The question that many non-Quakers ask is: what do Quakers believe? And a high proportion of questioners mean by this: Are Quakers Christian? The answer is that most, if not all, outside the UK would call themselves Christian, but in the UK things tend to be different. (I speak here for myself and report only what I have seen and experienced in the UK).

Quakers owe a great debt to Christianity, and Quakerism was born out of it but that does not mean that to be a Quaker you have to be a Christian. After all, Christianity had its roots in Judaism but opened itself to new light in the form of the great Jewish rabbi and spiritual teacher, Jesus of Nazareth. Christianity has its roots in Judaism but is not to be identified with it.

As I understand it, Christianity bases itself on belief in the resurrection as a condition for being a Christian and also as a basis for morality. There is the (for me) extraordinary statement that 'Christ died for our sins'. There is the well-known hymn in which it is said: 'He died that we might be forgiven'. What sort of deity is it who would put a human being through the torture that Jesus went through to justify forgiving humanity, which the omnipotent creator of the universe could surely have done in the twinkling of an eye without such a terrible experience for Jesus (supposedly God's son).

I ask myself how many Quakers in the UK actually believe in the virgin birth, miracles, the resurrection and that Jesus of Nazareth was literally the Son of God and of the same substance as God, who was crucified to save every human being from their sins.

Returning to the main issue, it may well be that Quakers are in the advance guard of a new spirituality. This has been called secular spirituality, atheist spirituality and religious nonbelief. All these are acceptable to those of us who are nontheists with a recognised spiritual dimension to our lives. Many Quakers would prefer not to disturb the present situation in which a wide diversity of beliefs coexist under what is called a Universalist umbrella. And it may well be that this sort of diversity is the future shape of things and that might be a very good thing.

At present, there seem to be two main groups. There are the Quakers who fled the Church of England (or other denomination) because of its liturgy, beliefs and practices, which had lost their meaning for them. On the other hand, there are those Quakers who see ourselves as part of the universe and, as Alex Wildwood put it: 'the unfolding self-realisation of a cosmic evolutionary process discovering, giving voice to, itself.'

Quakers and God

The relationship of Quakers to God is much the same as the relationship to Christianity. As you might expect, many find it unacceptable to think of someone calling her/himself a Quaker and a nontheist. It must be acknowledged, however, that *Quaker Faith and Practice* (a basic work for Quakers) leaves it open for the word 'God' to mean whatever one feels appropriate.

It would be helpful, I think, to quote here from study material issued in 2010 by the Woodbrooke Quaker Study Centre: 'There is great variety among Quakers in the ways we conceive of and experience God, and the different kinds of language we use to describe religious experience. Some Quakers have a conception of God which is similar to that of orthodox Christians, and would use similar language. Others are happy to use God-centred language, but would conceive of God in very different terms to the traditional Christian trinity. Some describe themselves as agnostics , or humanists, or non-theists and describe their experiences in ways that avoid the use of the word God entirely.' (*Becoming Friends. Living and learning with Quakers,* p.221).

It is also the case that most Quakers in the UK do not

have an idea of God as an 'entity' and would agree that the notion of God has changed over many years from a ferocious, revengeful tribal deity through loving father to something very different from a powerful person up in the sky. Some of these would take the view that God has existed through infinite time and remains the same throughout and it is human understanding which has evolved. My own view is that God is a human construct, whose particular form is a function of human social and individual circumstances which develops and changes with those circumstances. In other words, humanity creates God in its own image.

There is so much discussion surrounding this at present that it is impossible to predict what will happen. Diversity within Quaker unity will probably be accepted by the majority and we shall all go forward together and make a contribution to spiritual consciousness in the world out of all proportion to our small numbers.

Chapter 2

The Self-Referring Universe

After two years as an Attender, I became a Quaker in November 2004. It is well within the spirit of Quaker(ism) to move freely in one's intellectual and spiritual journey and I did just that. And my big 'leap forward' did not, as might be expected, originate in the spiritual sphere but came as a result of thinking about the universe and our place in it. I based my thinking on what I had read recently in semi-popular books on cosmology or astrophysics and what I remembered from my undergraduate days. Perhaps God was a huge question mark at the very back of my mind but this notion (of God) was really only a reminder of what other people thought.

I came up with some ideas quite soon that took me a step or two along what I know now to be my spiritual road. These ideas were based upon whatever scientific understanding and knowledge I had but because they related to the cosmos and our place in it and relationship to it, they had a transformative spiritual content. I had not set out with this intention. It just happened.

My starting point was the fact that even though we walk about and seem to be separate from other things, we are actually an integral part of the physical universe.

However, we are a conscious part of that universe. And all consciousness is an emergent property of the material world organised in a suitable way. Moreover, all our awareness is directed to some aspect of the universe, either the material world or the world of ideas and emotions. So each of us is a part of the universe relating in some way to another part of the universe. In other words, each of us is the universe becoming increasingly aware of itself. The universe, therefore, has a self-referential aspect. What does 'self-referential' mean? The meaning can seem quite complicated but it can also be seen simply if we are not too fussy about the explanation.

A 'self-referring' system is one which refers to itself. Strictly speaking, if it is self-referring, then it is closed. If the universe were infinite, it would be 'open', not closed. Is the universe as a whole infinite and open or is it self-referring and closed? It is difficult at present to get a definitive answer to this question. Fortunately, it scarcely matters under most circumstances because the universe in which we reside and which we experience is actually self-referring. Finite, unbounded and self-referring might be the best description. It is finite in the sense that wherever we are, it is in a finite place. We can never get to infinity or be 'at infinity'. The universe is unbounded in the sense that we never reach a boundary nor are we likely to. And it is self-referring because everything we (as the universe) relate to is the universe itself in some form. It behaves *as if* it were self-referring.

Am I inside or outside the universe? From a physical scientific viewpoint, everything is moving away from us and the farther it is away, the faster it is going. Paradoxically, if we were to view the universe from another galaxy we would still see everything moving away from us in the same way. So no point in our universe is special and certainly not the point we are at. We have no idea where we are! Yet, from another viewpoint, when I stand back and consider this it feels as if I were separate from the physical universe, looking at it from the outside, (on a line perpendicular to it as a mathematician might understand it). Yet I am the universe, an integral part of it. It feels as if consciousness is on a different sort of dimension from the three that we are familiar with.

We can develop upon this by looking at what happens when we perceive an object in the material world. The information about it (the light from it) arrives at our visual mechanism and brain, which processes it and decides on some response in the light of the information received. After responding, the object is viewed again by the perceptive mechanism to assess the effectiveness of the response. If the desired response has been achieved no correction is needed, but if a correction is needed the whole procedure is repeated. What is notable is that the perceptive mechanism which receives the initial information is, itself, part of the external material world which is being perceived and acted upon. The whole procedure is *self*-referential. The universe is relating to itself. The universe is the origin of the process and reflects back on itself.

This corresponds to the self-reference inherent in the linguistic tangle involved in the following:

Let S be the sentence which is defined by:

S: {The sentence S is false}

Curiously, you can say: If sentence S is true, then sentence S is false. (That is because what is in the curly brackets says this).

If sentence S is false, then sentence S is true. (This is because sentence S is true if what is said in the curly brackets is false).

In this tangle, sentence S is both subject and object.

This is like a Möbius strip, a long strip, one of whose ends is turned through 180 degrees before sticking the ends together. If you trace along this strip lengthwise you cover the entire length and end up at the point at which you started. The strip has no beginning and no end, no outside and no inside. This is like the sentence S because the latter refers to itself and has no real beginning and no real end. Subject and object are confused. Sentence S is the subject and it refers to itself as the object.

The difficulty is a linguistic one. Language is logical-linear; a sentence has a subject and a separate object, a beginning and an end. Perception, the self-referring sentence and the Möbius strip are all self-referring.

In looking at the universe, it appears perfectly linear (except for the curved space on a very large scale emerging from the general theory of relativity). This suggests that, like a Möbius strip, space is locally linear everywhere but curved and self-referring on a very large scale. We might be reminded of the pictorial work of M. C. Escher which has similar characteristics. The problem with anything self-referring, whether it is a Möbius strip or space, is that one does not know where to begin. But this is, in a very real sense, what makes it 'non-hierarchical'.

From a totally different perspective, the social zone, we might notice that the establishment, through the media and other means, distorts the self-reference of the universe into a linear-hierarchical form. Everything is presented as if it is linear-hierarchical, whereas many aspects of the cosmos at every level exhibit a self-referring character. Everything is presented as if there were always an order in which things happen and an order in which entities exist, including human beings. This order is one in which there is higher and lower, superior and inferior. Self-reference abolishes hierarchy as there is no beginning and no end.

People in Relation to the Self-Referring Universe

A question arises from the idea of self-reference. First, since inside and outside are relative, we might ask: Is the 'light' (as Quakers refer to it, or 'human spirit' as I prefer to call it) in you external to me? Or is it internal? The answer is that an aspect of what I see in you must be common to both of us because each of us emerges from the same cosmos. In looking at each other we each see a spirit which is particularised by the individual.

An extra bonus from this model is the unitary nature of humanity. Whatever 'light' I (as a conscious part of the universe), see in you, is also channelled through me to you. We are one-and-the-same at this level. I look at you and see me, in a special sense. And the same is true for you.

As Meister Eckhart put it: 'The eye through which I see God is the same as the eye through which God sees me.' As a nontheist, I translate this into: 'The eye through which I see the universe (or any part of it) is the same as the eye through which the universe sees me.'

The self-referential character of things suggests the absence of an 'outside' or an 'inside' to the universe. So, every point is simultaneously on the centre and the circumference and that includes every individual. It is not really possible at this level and in these terms to distinguish beginnings and ends, causes and effects.

And the self-reference of perception enables us to see it as a spiral, not a series of circles, because there is a continual progression, a correction to the circle of 'perceiving and acting upon'. And, intriguingly, spirals (mathematically known as helices) are found at every level of the universe – not only perception but galaxies, which are in spiral form; and ammonites, which are fossils in spiral form and DNA, which is in the form of a double helix.

Returning to the main issue: when I reflect upon anything, I am the universe becoming aware of itself because all reflection is relative to the universe. When I reflect upon myself reflecting, then perhaps, I (the subject) become identified with the object. At one level, subject and object are always identical because the universe is always both subject and object – anything else is not possible.

More than that, I, a small part of the conscious universe can think of (encompass) the whole. We are reminded of Blake:

'To see the world in a grain of sand,
And a heaven in a wild flower
Hold infinity in the palm of your hand;
And eternity in an hour.'

I do not physically contain the universe in my (partial) consciousness, but I map the whole universe in my consciousness. The whole encompasses/is contained in the part (in fact in each part) and vice versa. As far as you and I are concerned, my consciousness 'encompasses' yours and your consciousness 'encompasses' mine. This distinguishes mind/spirit – that is the non-material –from the material world. In the latter, taken by itself, the whole is equal to the sum of the parts, which is the case in a purely quantitative situation which has no basis for quality or the non-material.

Moreover, the mathematics of the infinite supports such a theory. It may be shown that the number of points on the smallest portion of a straight line are in one-to-one correspondence with the number of points in the entire universe. (See Chapter 4, below, p.98). [For more details, see Michael Talbot, *The Holographic Universe,* Harper Collins, 1996].

This very simplistic approach is reminiscent of the much more detailed and precisely formulated views of certain scientists such as David Bohm and Karl Pribram who have persuasively suggested that the universe is a hologram, a three-dimensional projection of a complicated web of interconnected fields. (This links with what has been said very recently on TV about the Higgs boson. See below in Chapter 5, p.126) This latter implicate order unfolds into the explicate order that we know. They suggest that the universe is a hologram in which the smallest part contains the whole and a small 'whole' contains any much larger 'whole'.

The Self-Referring Universe and the Search for Meaning

The universe is self-referring and I am part of the universe, a conscious part. And everything I am aware of relates to some aspect of the universe. Thus, I am the universe becoming increasingly aware of itself. From this we can make an inference which has reassuring implications for the meaning of one's life. And the inference does not involve a transcendent deity.

Just as any person's thinking/feeling/emotion contributes to the development of the individual as a person, for either good or ill, so the thinking/feeling/emotion of any part of the universe must contribute to the development of the universe, for either good or ill. And each of us is a part of the universe. So for each of us, it is the case that our feelings, thoughts and emotions contribute to the development of the entire universe. A strange thought, perhaps? In short, all our experiences contribute to the development of the universe, to transforming it in some way.

The objection may be made that this applies only to the part of the universe in which a person doing the experiencing *is*. Perhaps so. I prefer to think that the universe resembles a human being. When a human being develops through experience, we do not think that only the conscious part of the person changes. The person *as a whole* (including arms and legs and so on) is thought of as participating in this. We are brought by this to a rather reassuring idea and that is that for any conscious being, any experience/feeling/thought /emotion contributes to the development of the cosmos and this is so however short the life of the individual concerned and whatever form such experience takes.

Even uncommunicated thoughts and emotions make their contribution. Nothing is wasted – at least at the cosmic level. This is not to say that at the social, experiential level, there is no such waste. Far from it. The wastage there is appalling. Millions of people live lives that involve them to such an extent in the struggle for survival that nothing is left over. And that is to omit mention of untimely death due to poverty, lack of medical facilities and wars.

But in the final analysis, at the cosmic level, there is no waste – a situation which seems far superior to the one the religious authorities present. Their picture is of a universe presided over by an omniscient, omnipotent being allowing untold cruelty, barbarism and the waste of millions of lives, the vast majority of the world's population. Who are the humanists here?

It is often said by nontheists or agnostics that there is no need for a heaven because we live on in the memories of those we leave behind. Alternatively, our immortality consists in our achievements in this world. But suppose no one remembers us for very long?

Suppose we have no notable achievements? It is not surprising that many people need the reassurance of the hope of an afterlife to give meaning to their lives as experienced here.

The problem of meaning (albeit in a rather abstract way) is solved decisively by the model proposed here. In this scenario we contribute involuntarily every moment of our lives whether we like it or not and whether we know it or not. Meaning is a given, an amazing gift out of the generosity of the universe itself. That is the way things are.

Perhaps this picture is simplistic and over-optimistic but it does make sense in another and, perhaps, more simplistic way. For, in the developing process which is the universe, if each of us plays our role, then that role will make a contribution, for good or evil. Banal though it may sound, this tells me that I must try to maximise my influence for good in this development. I must put my shoulder to the wheel in the cosmic battle between good and evil by maximising the 'good' side (as I see it) through my thoughts and actions. It is not appropriate to start going into the question of what is good and what is evil at this point if only because the issue is too large, too deep and too important to deal with here. It certainly has an aspect of relativity and, at the same time, there is its absolute aspect which is the experiential, practical effect of any thought or action. To take a banal but obvious example: Hitler must have thought the Holocaust was a good thing. We would all assert that it manifested absolute evil.

I know that my perception of what is right/good and

what is wrong/bad is just that – my own perception. However, I have to hope I am not too far out and act for the good as far as possible. The meaning of my life has thus become cosmic and this is right down to the smallest action I take and the most fleeting thought. And this applies to every single person in the world. It follows immediately that the very existence of the universe provides an ultimate basis for morality and there is no need for different religions to intervene in order to claim the credit for this.

As I write this, I wonder if, in fact, a reflection upon all this is not even more transformative than the action or thought itself.

Even a simple perception does not mean simply going round in circles of self-reference but proceeding in 'spirals' of self-correction and transformation. And the creative aspect arises from the fact that it is only in the presence of the 'perceiver' that the connections are made and relationships set up which result in a sequence of such perceptions. The clap of thunder is only a noise because someone is there to receive the waves stimulating the hearing mechanism.

Special cases

It is possible to see certain everyday phenomena a bit differently on the basis of a self-referential universe. We start from the undoubted fact that I am the universe becoming aware of itself. That is general. Let us look at some special cases.

What is a mathematician? A mathematician is the universe becoming aware of its own structure.

What is a Quaker Meeting? A Quaker Meeting is the universe contemplating its own essence/core/heart /centre.

What is a philosopher? A philosopher is the universe becoming aware of the connections between itself as subject and itself as object.

What is a composer? A composer is the universe expressing and re-creating itself in sounds.

What is a painter? A painter is the universe expressing and re-creating itself in light.

What is a scientist? A scientist is the universe becoming aware of its own mechanism.

What is a historian? A historian is the universe becoming aware of its own past.

What is a teacher? A teacher is the universe trying to enable another part of the universe to see itself more clearly and become more aware of itself.

What is a poet? A poet is the universe re-creating itself by permuting different ways of seeing itself.

What is a novelist? A novelist is the universe creating new universes out of itself by rearranging its components.

What is a dancer? A dancer is the universe copying itself. (Assuming, as some would see it, that the universe consists of the dances of a wide variety of energies).

What is an executioner? An executioner is the universe destroying its own consciousness, that is, committing suicide.

Finally, we may ask: 'What is the idea of God?' The

answer to this was briefly referred to in the previous chapter (pp.19-20) but it calls for expansion. The answer, from an individual point of view, is: A person's concept of God *ideally* is the abstraction of what there is in common between all the abstractions from all the examples of that person's particular experience of infinitude, beauty, goodness, truth, love, omnipotence and so on. To make this clearer: my idea of beauty is gained by abstracting from all the particular examples of beautiful things I have experienced. My idea of truth is gained by abstracting from all the particular examples of truth I have experienced. And so on for the others. When I take all these abstract ideas from each particular characteristic (of beauty, truth and so on) and abstract that which is common to all of them, I arrive at the idea of God. In other words, God is not simply an abstract concept but a 'doubly abstract' concept.

When looked at from a cosmic viewpoint we have to say that God is the universe trying to account for and make sense of its own existence, using its conscious aspects to perform the previous double abstraction in order to do this.

Unsurprisingly, this is also true of the concept of number. (See below, pp.91-2 for detailed discussion). This is so because all our ideas and perceptions have some form of objective basis, however much 'rearranged'. We are as much constrained by objective phenomena in constructing a concept of God (or number) as with anything else.

Actor and Audience

A major problem with respect to all this is that, in order to relate to anything whatsoever, you have to be separate from it, not part of it. As we are part of the universe relating to itself we always have to 'distance' ourselves from that which is being perceived or cognised. It must surely be the function of our material universe existing in terms of space and time to enable us to do this. There are even special neurones which enable us to perceive 'borders' to things.

Nevertheless, we are still in the position of being simultaneously actor and audience in the great drama that is being played out. This means oscillating rapidly from subject to object as we reflect upon things existing and happening. This is self-reference applied to oneself and its disadvantage is that, in reflecting upon oneself, it is hard not to be self-conscious. It is a marvellous thing for the universe to be able to do – to reflect upon itself reflecting upon itself. Perhaps this is the sort of development which is a primary purpose of the universe of which we are a part.

In summary then, we (the universe) relate to a cosmos which is organised so that we are able to separate ourselves from it (in thought only) and see it as composed of solid objects which, themselves, are separate from each other. Thus, we can relate to the universe by means of a mechanism which is part of it but can behave *as if* we are separate. And this applies not only to the physical universe but to the social milieu as well.

Babies are born into social milieu which programme them into constructing a model of the world, material, individual and social, which provides a basic conditioning which none of us can grow out of. The acceptance of such a model is the price we pay for the protection of society when we are totally helpless. The variations in such models correspond to the diverse cultures into which we are born. Our immense adaptability enables the human infant to be programmed into a wide variety of different models. Helplessness and adaptability - the two sides of the general nature of the human infant that are decisively formative, positively and negatively. This may work very well in babyhood but it becomes an obstacle to development in later life, when the adult is no longer really helpless. We all know how easy it is to be too adaptable.

Nevertheless, the variety of cultures which we manifest plays an important part in enabling the universe to have a wide variety of experiences as it becomes (through us as individuals) more and more aware of itself and its possibilities. In fact, the universe has sufficient imagination to construct a wide variety of different gods as each culture seems to have its own. There seems to be no limit to the variety of gods which may be constructed, each suitable (obviously) to the culture out of which it has grown.

We are all part of the mystery we are trying to solve (self-referentially) and we learn to behave as if separate from our different milieux in order to be in some sense 'outside' the process. Only thus can we begin to relate to the process of which we are a part. 'Be ye in the world but not of it', said Jesus and as far as our consciousness is concerned, we cannot do anything else. It is enormously more difficult to carry this out in the social sphere, which was what he was talking about. And this is what makes self-transformation (and the consequent transformation of society) so difficult to achieve. We are fortunate that a multitude of factors conspire to make this happen in spite of our woeful inadequacies.

The above account of how I acquired a picture of our universe and our place in it is, of necessity, a 'smoothed out' one. It might be called a 'logical reconstruction'. However, that is how it appears with hindsight, as such things do. The logic of such a model seems to me (at present) to be inescapable, based as it is on what I think to be the case – that is, that for which there appears to be scientific evidence. Science, however, does not stand still, it constantly moves on as new technology brings to light so much that was hitherto unknown. And as such knowledge comes to light and natural science changes and develops, one's ideas must change in correspondence with it.

There is no problem in this as an unlimited number of 'logics' may apply to the same situation. So I also realise that, at this very moment, someone with the same basic knowledge might well come up with a different model from mine. This is all right providing they do not try to force it upon anybody else. What is certain for me, however, is that I shall never look at the situation as I see it and then make a 'leap' from that situation to a totally different zone of existence – that which is disconnected with the material universe and is said to transcend it. This brings me to the next chapter which discusses such anomalies often found in the thinking of theist scientists.

Chapter 3

God as a Product of the Human Spirit

There is a relatively little-known story about Napoleon and the great eighteenth century mathematician Pierre-Simon de Laplace (1749 - 1827). After reading Laplace's monumental work *Traité de* méchanique *céleste* (Celestial Mechanics), Napoleon asked him: 'Where is the place of God in all this?' Laplace replied: 'Je n'ais pas besoin de cette hypothèse.' ('I have no need of such a hypothesis.'). This was certainly an acceptable logical point, which is not surprising as the work in question was a wonderful combination of formal logic together with the logic of mathematics.

However, the issue is not a black and white one, a matter of pure logic in which God is put forward as a hypothesis and the propositions (of religion) are seen as either true or false and, if necessary, are easily and unhesitatingly jettisoned. What has to be reckoned with is the fact that most of the millions of the world's masses, those who most need to liberate themselves, would find it hardest to dispense with the crutch afforded by their particular religion.

There is no need to repeat here the well-known reasons for atheism (nontheism) spelled out so cogently by so many able and erudite authors: Richard Dawkins,

Sam Harris, Christopher Hitchens and so on. Nor is there any need to refer yet again to the iniquitous behaviour of institutional religions, for example the Christian Inquisition, Muslim wars of conquest, Hindu massacres of Muslims and Hebrew expropriation of the lands of others at the bidding of the tribal God in the Old Testament. Not to mention the misogyny and homophobia of all three Abrahamic religions.

The majority of people would not necessarily be moved by having these facts pointed out to them because nobody is moved by an appeal to rationality alone. Life is much more than this, as we all know. It is messy, mixed-up, contradictory and emotional. Thoughts happen altogether and not in a neat logical chain of inference. This is true of everyone, myself included, so this chapter about God and religion is a sort of logical reconstruction of ideas and thoughts which occurred over the years since I became a Quaker. I had been a nontheist for decades but began to read and think properly about the issues involved quite late in life, despite believing that my mind was already made up. The result was a transformation in my understanding but not in my general conclusions. And I experienced a new spiritual freedom such as I had not known existed simply because my thinking was now on a new dimension.

One point needs clarification before proceeding. The reader will have noticed that the word nontheist has been used where the word atheist might have been expected. My reason for this is based mainly upon the fact that I have never had an experience of God. Here, a theist might rightly object that because something is not experienced it does not imply that it does not exist. In other words, lack of experience of God does not mean that God does not exist.

My answer to that objection is that if I am told that an entity exists of which I have no experience, then that entity may be anything or nothing. In this case, I put nothing in the space which the theist fills with God. If I were to insert anything at all, the insert would be totally arbitrary and, therefore, meaningless because of the absence (for me) of evidence.

I use the word nontheist sooner than atheist because I recognise the above argument and do not base my belief-system on the existence of any form of deity. At the end of the road, though, each of us has the right to describe ourselves as we please. If any one of us were asked, 'What is an atheist?', or 'What is a nontheist?', hopefully we would reply as Marx's friend Engels did: 'Someone who sees the world without any transcendental admixture'.

Thinking about God

If you want to think something out afresh you cannot do better than try to empty your mind of preconceptions and start from the beginning. Of course, this is ultimately an impossible task as there is that which cannot be emptied (conditioning, education, experiences, cultural influences, ways of looking at things and so forth) but it is well worth the effort and the results are certainly better than not trying at all and simply plodding on in the old ways. In considering the idea of God, there is no actual evidence to go on, so we have to do the best we can to think for ourselves. This is so, even though there are those who would strongly dispute the suggestion of there being no evidence. However, it cannot be bad to start out by trying to think things out for oneself.

The first question coming to mind is: what, if anything, is the idea of God about? In other words, if there were a God, what would it be? Surely it cannot be an entity, a sort of 'thing'? Since it would be transcendental it could not be material. Perhaps there is a non-material existent whose nature we cannot conceive of but which has its being beyond our comprehension? However, that brings us back to the God of the theists, that is, a God who, though totally without attributes providing evidence for existence, is provided with qualities such as being revengeful, jealous, loving or compassionate, according to the culture and historical period with which s/he is connected. If s/he were a principle and not an entity, then s/he could not be a creative power because a principle cannot act upon anything. Some people say that God is pure love but this is surely an avoidance of the issue? It is certainly difficult to know what this means. What about pure energy? A good idea, perhaps, but again too woolly, and on its own without any other external agent, not changeable into matter as Einstein's equation suggests it must be capable of.

Dilemmas about the existence or otherwise of God are normally solved by pre-empting the issue in some way. Many theists would assert that there must be *something* but the standard reply to this is that, if there is something, what preceded it? Or as many sensible children express it: if God created the universe, who created God?

Following this, we might be driven to ask: if the questions surrounding the existence of God are so difficult, why are there so many believers? The most important factor here is the deep conditioning undergone by hundreds of millions from an extremely early age; such conditioning being an intrinsic part of the customs of every society in some form or other. And the most significant transmitter of the conditioning is the family, usually the mother. For the helpless baby or very young child there is absolutely no escape.

It matters not whether such pressures involve unpleasant threats of dire punishment after death following upon disobedience to the rules and regulations laid down by the putative deity or whether the pressure is exerted in a much milder form. Such powerful pressures are almost impossible to remove altogether.

Following on the situation in which the family is the principal instrument, the religious institutions in the form of the religious authorities step in later and customs and public and private ceremonies do their part. Vast amounts have been written on religion, its history and sociology, the religious customs of different cultures throughout the ages and in different parts of the globe. It is neither necessary nor possible to deal with any of this here. The family does its part from the earliest part of life as the agent of the establishment and the greater society is ready to add to this later on. And amongst the weapons used to enslave the individual for life, the most effective one is guilt. Nothing is more liable to render the individual helpless and at the mercy of the established society in which he or she lives than early and deeply embedded guilt. This has been stated generally because it is still the case in the majority of cultures. It is only in a tiny minority of families in enlightened situations that the situation is moderated by liberal values.

Despite all the family and social pressures on the individual, however, people have constantly rebelled and reason and emotion have combined to assert the freedom of the human spirit. Therefore, it is not surprising that, over the centuries, for hundreds of years, a large number of arguments have had to be advanced for the existence of God. And it is interesting and amusing to note that, as God is made in the image of man, the type of argument used in such proofs reveals the different images of God obtaining under different circumstances.

You only have to go to the web to discover immediately the enormous number of proofs of the existence of God that there are. In the medieval world the scholastic philosophers produced a number of 'logical' arguments of which two are typical. First, the ontological argument: If God exists he must be perfect. One of the qualities of perfection is existence. Therefore, God must exist. Then there is the cosmological argument: Everything that exists must have a cause. The universe exists. Therefore God exists.

Such proofs have had their day but highly intelligent people constructed such proofs and, presumably, believed in them. God is seen as a subject of a logical category. Nothing could be more abstract and remote from the popular God of the Old and New Testaments than the God of the medieval philosophers. The problem is how they managed to grasp the two sorts of God simultaneously.

Today, especially in our own society in the West, things are as one would expect. The presentation is normally in terms of the opposition of science and religion and especially in terms of the opposition of the theory of evolution on one hand and the idea of intelligent design on the other. Unfortunately, such opposition is usually presented as *either* pure chance *or* 'intelligent design', where intelligent design is interpreted as by the hand of God. Evolution is presented as a result of chance mutations and intelligent design as the result of a purposeful God. Such a dualistic presentation allows for no other possibility.

Just as in media presentations of a host of other problems such as political decisions, the issue is presented dualistically, that is, as an 'either – or' situation. In this way, the preferred option of the powers-that-be is presented in contrast to one other totally unacceptable possibility. Such was the case during the Cold War, for example. Without anyone plotting to do so, this is a remarkably effective way of inveigling the population into thinking in establishment terms.

It is so much more appealing to think of humanity as the product of the intentions of an all-powerful creator who loves each one of us individually than to see ourselves as the result of chance mutations at the microscopic level whom absolutely no one cares about, tiny and alone in an unimaginably large cosmos.

There are, though, other alternatives. It cannot be simply a case of either intelligent design alone or chance alone. What happens in the universe is not merely a matter of chance. We do not need science to tell us that – it is obvious from experience that, as well as chance, there are various causal factors at work at a variety of different levels. And recent results confirm that it is intrinsic to the emergence of processes in nature that the element of *self*-determination becomes more and more prominent as the process develops.

The notion of intelligent design opens the door wide to creationism because the very word 'design' itself presupposes a designer. We easily build models corresponding to our own experience. And our own experience points to a producer when we encounter a product. We do not, normally, look for another, more sophisticated explanation as we are, on the whole, rather lazy mentally and are also deeply set in our ways. That is, we are deeply involved in our own conditioning. The force of habit is a powerful force, as Vladimir Lenin once wrote.

Theist Arguments

An issue much stressed by theists, especially scientists, is the so-called anthropic principle. It seems that, for the universe to be as it is, and that means including life and consciousness, the fundamental physical constants have to be precisely determined. The physical constants are such numbers as the ratio of the mass of the proton to that of the electron, the numerical value of the force of gravity at any point and so on. These have to have very special and incredibly precise values, otherwise there would be no life and, therefore, we would not be here to tell the tale. The probability of these constants having the precise values needed for the existence of life is very small indeed.

Thus, say the scientist-theists, design is more than suggested, it is incredibly highly probable. It is almost impossible that our universe with its population of living and also conscious beings could have come into existence by pure chance. They conclude that the only possible explanation for the existence of everything, including ourselves, is a deity, a creator, with the necessary culturally-determined attributes, according to the background of the particular believer involved. George Ellis calls this the basic theological view. He argues brilliantly and persuasively (in *Before the Beginning*, p.110ff) that science, and physics in particular, cannot explain everything, and in this he is perfectly right. However, his dazzling and erudite arguments conceal a logical hiatus. There is a tiny (but infinitely significant) gap between his scientific and theological zones as he makes a totally unacceptable 'leap' to prefer the existence of a deity.

Ellis also argues that this does not in any way contradict the findings of science but he is still not justified in falling back upon a logical hiatus. You cannot leap from the anthropic principle to a theological solution. If you start from the realm of science there is, in fact, no way of seamlessly moving into the realm of the theological. There is, however, another possible nontheist resolution of the problem posed by the anthropic principle. Everything, material or non-material, is in a permanent state of flux. Our own universe is no exception and may be seen as a monumental pulsation, expanding now but probably fated to contract to nothing in due course. If time is infinite, our universe may well be the most recent in a long line of universes which have expanded and contracted to nothing. If so, then each of these universes would have had its own constants, which might or might not have led to the evolution of intelligent life. It is a distinct possibility that our universe is the one, after countless others, which has had the very constants facilitating our emergence. We may even be optimistic and hope that, if this is the case, then when our universe has contracted to nothing eventually, a future possible universe will be born which will not only have the right numerical constants for intelligent life, it will do better than that. Perhaps such intelligent life will lead to a consciousness far superior to ours, in which living beings will not exploit, oppress, torture or kill one another for private gain or for the sake of mere power for themselves.

The most unappealing theist argument is one that does not need a scientific advocate and that is the idea that the reason that some people are atheists is that they do not work hard enough at cultivating a spiritual sense. Such hard work would enable us to have some experience of God, it is suggested. Even Karen Armstrong (*The Case for God: What Religion Really Means*, p.4) suggests that 'Like any skill, religion requires perseverance, hard work and discipline.' Even more depressing is her suggestion that: 'Some people will be better at it than others, some appallingly inept, and others will miss the point entirely.'

Not only is it depressing to think of all that hard work but there is the added deterrent of, perhaps, being one of those unfortunates who 'miss the point entirely.' Would this be better or worse than being 'appallingly inept'? Apparently God is not politically correct in his selection of those who benefit from spiritual experiences and many of us will be left behind in the race to love and be loved by this deity. How is it possible to see spirituality as a skill and spiritual experience to be achieved only as a result of special training and a great deal of practice? Even orthodox religionists tell of people like Joan of Arc whose 'experiences' were involuntary. I could never believe in or respect a God who was so elitist in his attitudes.

There are, however, other suggestions. The most appealing one comes from Paul Davies (*God and the New Physics*, p.223). While recognising the logical-mathematical structure of the universe, he suggests that this does not rule out a natural God as opposed to a supernatural one. While this argument is logically quite correct, it does not address the fact that a natural God becomes part of the natural universe and as well as being subject to the laws of that universe, it would be hard to attribute supernatural properties to him. In particular, it would be virtually impossible for institutional religion to emerge from such a conception. And establishments do need to be able to impose their concepts of God and religion on their populations. It is no accident that such a conception, that of a natural God, has been marginalised and treated as 'cranky'.

At the end of the road, though, this does not help in explicating the problem of 'beginnings' and 'ends' and we are no further forward. Furthermore, does 'natural' mean a part of the material universe or does it mean what the medieval philosophers termed 'immanent'?

There is one thing in common between the theists who are scientists and those who are not and this is that the existence of God is assumed in all of their arguments. The theists who are not scientists simply *pre*suppose such existence and the theists who are scientists '*post*suppose' it as George Ellis does (if the reader will excuse the shameless invention of a word with no previous existence). Furthermore, after such pre- or post-supposition, there is a free flow of assumptions about the nature of the deity: omnipotent, omniscient, loving, infinite, forgiving, compassionate and so forth. Today, in the era of multiculturalism there is also the assumption that the variety of gods worshipped by different people in different cultures are really all the same. And this despite a variety of often conflicting characteristics and accompanying rules and moralities.

I am led to wonder, 'If God existed, then the lack of evidence for his existence might be deliberate on his part and is merely a way of his testing our rationality and independence of mind. If he existed, he might want to test us in this way. So, if there were a God, I am doing the right thing and if there is not there is no problem at all.'

The idea of God is a concept which for many people

today is a highly abstract one, in fact a 'double abstraction' as was suggested in the previous chapter (p.33). It has been variously constructed by different people at different times under different circumstances and for different reasons. Early in human history it was fear of the very powerful forces their lives were subject to or it may have been the wish to placate those external forces on behalf of fertility or something similar. Later, it was a social God who was moralistic and finally, a cosmic spirit which embodies perfection, infinitude, unqualified love and so on.

Certainly, the earlier we go back, the less abstract it becomes and the socially-based, evolving God of human history is a real image of authority for the particular society involved.

If God is a concept like all others, then we creatively construct our image, and it is based on the normal objective constraints of social and individual spiritual experience. Thus, it is no surprise that it changes with time, place and circumstances. As David Boulton wrote in his marvellous book *The Trouble with God*, it is not God who grows up but human consciousness which matures. It is humankind that has moved its ideal from a frightening, revengeful tribal chief via a moral, loving father through to a cosmic spirit arising from the wholeness of the universe itself and with no other possible characteristics than being non-material.

Far from God being the ultimate creator, the concept of God has itself emerged from the material universe itself. It has necessarily arisen from the *relationships* between human beings and the various milieux inhabited by them as it is only *relationships* which constitute the universe's creative aspect.

The Universe and Self-Reference Again

It is a tribute to the human spirit that the concept of God has advanced as much as it has and in so doing has furthered the very development of the universe itself and the universe's own awareness of itself. However, it has logically led to its own rejection of itself by many for reasons which have been well documented elsewhere. And this is not always at all easy, especially in nonliberal cultures such as those embracing Islam. It is hard, too, for orthodox Jews, for similar, though less drastic reasons because there may be a form of excommunication in Judaism but there is no form of death sentence as there is in Islam. However, as has already been said, there are considerable difficulties for most people due to early indoctrination.

Moreover, we are all simultaneously godlike and human. Insofar as we 'construct' the world, we are godlike. However, we are subject to objective constraints and in that sense are simply human.

We can now begin to answer the question: what am I here for? Having no belief in an external creator, I have no sense that someone brought me into the world thinking: 'That's what Muriel is there for. Mind you, she has no way of knowing exactly and for sure what I have in mind for her but she is supposed to carry out my wishes anyway.'

What is certain is that we all grow out of the universe and are conscious parts or aspects of it. So the universe is conscious of itself because I, the universe, am conscious of different aspects of it. Every feeling I have, every thought, emotion, feeling of joy or anguish, is the universe becoming more aware of itself. My principal purpose in life is to contribute to this ongoing process. Every good action or idea or thought or emotion contributes to this as does all the evil. Since I want the good to triumph in the end, it is incumbent on me to think good thoughts and do good. I must support others, encourage them and do what is possible for their good and my own.

This may appear simplistic but it makes clear that there is no waste in the world – for each and every one of us, every aspect of our lives contributes to the development of the universe in one way or another. This happens whether we like it or not. We do this all the time unwittingly. We have no control over it. It happens through our contribution to the universe's awareness of itself and our contribution to the eternal battle between good and evil.

And this has to be true of everyone without exception – even Hitler. In case anyone cannot stomach this (and there must be many such) it must be pointed out that Hitler had relationships which were not inherently evil – with his dog, for example or to Eva Braun. On the other hand, Hitler's relationship to me and hundreds of millions of others far outweighed these in effect and there can be no doubt that he contributed massively to the evil in the universe.

And it cannot be said that Hitler the man was good

but he did bad things, as I have heard suggested. Each of us exists exclusively through our relationships and not as 'things' in isolation. Some of our relationships are 'good' or 'positive' and this accounts for the aspect of us that is to be cherished. Other relationships are not so good and may even, on occasion, be undesirable and even 'bad'. When Quakers say that 'there is good/God in everyone' this does not mean that everyone is exclusively good. It means that we should look out for and base ourselves on the good. This saying refers to individuals and is not relevant at the social level to collections of people.

Religion and Science

Most of the time, the majority of people are too overwhelmed by the necessity of making a living and surviving in this disgracefully unjust, poverty-stricken world to worry about the really big issues. But right down deep these questions are always there waiting to be answered and, especially at climactic times in life, they become overwhelmingly important.

The big, unanswered (and unanswerable?) questions are very simple: Why am I here? What is the point of it all? Why are things as they are? Why is there anything at all? What is it all for? Why bother with anything? Another might be: How does it come about that there is such an enthralling contradiction between the fact that everything around us seems perfectly natural and normal and yet, at the same time, it is entirely miraculous that it should be the case?

Surely everyone has thought along these lines at some time or another in their lives? It does not need any sophistication to do so. Our apparent inability to produce any satisfactory answers opens the door for religious solutions to humanity's worries and dilemmas. Certainly, no scientist would suggest that there is any sort of scientific answer to these questions.

However, there are other big questions which correspond to them and which may be posed in a scientific form: Why do the laws of nature have the form that they have? Why does the model of the material universe consist of such things as atoms and molecules and other such entities? How did such things emerge from nothing (apparently)? How did atoms and molecules and such things get organised into organic living beings? How did the universe get started? Will the universe come to an end and how will this happen? What is the purpose of the universe? What has this got to do with me?

Some of these, the 'How?' questions, come within the realm of scientific investigation but even though they refer to scientific objects others, the 'Why?' questions, do not. And the two final questions dealing with purpose and the role of human beings in the cosmos, which are also basically 'Why?' questions even though they are framed in different words, are also beyond the possibility of scientific investigation.

What is it that makes a 'How?' question scientific but not the other sort? The most important criterion is testability, the possibility of verifying and of falsifying. This implies that the testing has a public dimension.

Which means that experiments have to be repeatable and also that predictions can be made.

It also means that such questions as that pertaining to the origin of the universe in its 'How?' form are on the borders of the scientific domain because the tests which verify the results have to be very sophisticated indeed and, in actuality, only falsification is (relatively) reliable. Perhaps we are reaching the limits of what may be called 'science'?

We must grant this and also grant that, as cosmology advances and retreats further from us in distance as well as in time, it becomes more and more difficult to verify or falsify the results of experiments or inferences from them. Nevertheless, over a very wide range of questions, it still remains that the domain of science is distinguishable from that of religion or philosophy. The domain of the scientific can be distinguished by the possibility of objective testing.

The scientific domain is not static by any means but, as the cosmological example shows, is liable to change itself. And not only is the domain of the scientific in constant change, every experimental result is only valid within a certain domain. And it is only possible to know the domain for which a particular result holds after having gone to the limit and found the so-called scientific law falsified.

Here we arrive at the most significant thing that distinguishes science from religion – its provisional, relative character. All scientific results are liable to be overthrown. If they haven't been yet, then we eagerly await such a situation. Every experiment, together with its result, is an absolute but the law formulated as an abstraction from such results is relative. Not only does the content of science differ from that of religion but also its entire methodology and expectations. Whoever heard of a religion which intrinsically involved the overturning of its beliefs if they were queriable?

All the more strange is it, then, that there are theists who would query this and who would speak of a 'science of religion'. Ken Wilber (*Quantum Questions*, p.20) says that religion may be called a science because there is religious experience. Such experience is not private but public because we can train our consciousness, through meditation or contemplation, to apprehend the zone of religious experience (soul or spirit). The public nature of our religious consciousness derives from such training.

So we can speak of the science of religion, says Wilber, because the domains of the soul or spirit are public (or shareable or intersubjective). How can this be? What is experienced by the soul or spirit is not shareable for the simple reason that there is no way of testing/measuring the experiences of the soul or spirit. Nor is there a means of predicting what future experiences will be. And uninspiring though they may be, these are the tests of public, shareable science - the possibility of common measurements and of verifiable predictions.

Why even try to present religion as a science? Surely its great strength is that it is *not* reducible to testability and predictiveness in this way? And in speaking of religion I do not mean to imply that a religious attitude involves a belief in a deity because it does not. 'Religious' is referred to here as Einstein referred to it when he called himself 'a religious unbeliever'. A religious attitude to the world and to life implies a deep sense of curiosity and a profound sense of wonder in the face of the marvels, beauties and harmonies which can be uncovered by the hard-working scientist or revealed by the gifted artist, painter or composer.

Perhaps the reason for trying to identify religion with science is that it would mean that the experiences of religious people could then be treated as if they were tried and tested scientific 'facts'? They would thereby gain the status and claim the credentials of science as well as having the unassailability of private belief.

Religion and Social Control

Perhaps that sort of question and implied judgement is too harsh in an individual case, and it may well be that the person concerned is passionate about both his religious beliefs and physics and is desperate to bring them together. There may well be many people in this frame of mind for whom a logical approach to the issue is inadequate. I was reminded of this possibility when re-reading this wonderful quotation from Karl Marx's *Contribution to the Critique of Hegel's Philosophy of Right,* given in Christopher Hitchens, *The Portable Atheist,*

> '*Religious* distress is at the same time the *expression* of real distress and the *protest* against

> real distress. Religion is the sigh of the oppressed masses, the heart of a heartless world, just as it is the spirit of a spiritless situation. It is the *opium* of the people.
>
> The abolition of religion as the *illusory* happiness of the people is required for their *real* happiness. The demand to give up the illusions about its condition is the *demand to give up a condition which needs illusions.* The criticism of religion is therefore *in embryo the criticism of the vale of woe,* the *halo* of which is religion.'

The humanity in this comes as a great surprise to most people, conditioned as they are to viewing Marxism as bigoted, cold, mechanistic and falsely analytical. It *is* analytical and powerfully and correctly so. It hits the spot unerringly when it sees that the demand to do away with the illusions of religion is the same as the demand to do away with the conditions which give rise to the need for such illusions. Marx sees the misery of the conditions under which people live as giving rise to the need for consolation and comfort which religion, it must be admitted, can give like nothing else.

Although it is not spelled out, the implication is that Marx is referring to social conditions and may not have individual tragedy and sadness in mind. What he says is applicable, though, to individual as well as social misery. So the issue is not a black-and-white one, a matter of pure logic in which the propositions of religion are seen as either true or false and, having been seen to be false, are easily and unhesitatingly jettisoned. What has to be reckoned with is the fact that most of the millions of the world's masses, those who most need to liberate themselves, would find it hardest to dispense with the crutch afforded by their particular religion.

It would be all too easy in our twenty-first century Western society to belittle the problem of the gullibility of masses of people who much too easily believe what is told them by authorities (and not only by religious authorities). It might seem an easy task to disabuse people of their illusions simply by telling them about the nature of the universe which physical science has uncovered over the past four hundred years or so, and about the methods of science which demand evidence and the testing of results and humanity's ability to change the world by means of the applications of scientific theory.

It is not as easy as that. People are not convinced by such a line of argument if their deepest emotions are involved. We know this in respect of other forms of belief – for example political beliefs. Hundreds of millions of people are sorely oppressed by the effects of capitalism and feudalism but make no effort to change the situation. Nor are they prepared to accept that there is an acceptable alternative. They see the existing situation as the natural order of things. And we know that much hard experience is necessary before people are prepared to take matters into their own hands and their fate under their own control. Even then, they may exchange one bad situation for another which is just as bad but different. People need to be full of fury at their oppressors before they rebel and even then they often calm down all too quickly and opt again for the quiet life.

We know how difficult change of mind is with respect to politics and yet we tend to think it should be relatively easy with religious belief. We do not treat such beliefs with the same degree of seriousness as political beliefs. Worse than that, religion is usually given privileged status, not only by the establishment but also by ordinary people who collude in the cushioning of religion against the totally justified right of people to criticise ideas.

A major problem consists in the fact that we are conditioned from birth to make one of these religions our own and it is hard to shake off such indoctrination. We take it in with the earliest conditioning to cultural norms. We are born as helpless babies who are, nevertheless, supremely adaptable and so we adapt to the society we are born into because if we do not do so we would die. We do it to survive. We learn very early that in order to survive we have to adapt to our environment. We learn this lesson from early on and as it seems to work we keep doing it. And we go on surviving so that proves that adaptation and survival go together. From then on, the social establishment has really won the game. It takes heroic efforts to overcome this and to try and stand on one's own feet.

We adapt to the religious milieu and assume that our identity is what we are told. 'We are Jewish'. 'We are Christian'. Or 'We are Muslims'. How can a baby have any religious identity? The answer to this is obvious, but the reality of associating one's personal identity with the religion of one's parents is very difficult to shake off. And later on in life, there is so much to lose – family, friends, safety, support and familiar, repeated customs. It is no wonder that so many sceptics take the easy road and just keep their own counsel about their actual feelings. Of course it is not the same with political beliefs. In most families, no one would consider it a capital crime for a son or daughter to vote differently from their parents.

This is why religion has been so useful to establishments in reinforcing social control. Not only has it the backing of divine authority in proclaiming rules and regulations for living which render the population powerless and subservient, but it provides words of comfort at times of greatest stress and anguish for individual people. And these functions are not necessarily performed in a mechanistic way but they often interpenetrate each other so that the captivity of the individual human spirit is as complete as possible.

'Slaves obey your masters'. 'Women obey your husbands'.

'The monarch is God's anointed'. Customs which are often tribal in origin are taken up and given a religious edge to provide them with unquestionable authority. When the law says that women and men must not be in the same room together alone, or that a woman may not leave the house without a male relative accompanying her or forbids women to drive, it may look like totally irrational backwardness. These rules and others such as monstrous dress codes actually have a practical origin in the property relations of early societies. They arise originally from the fear of adultery which may lead to property going to a child who is not the man's own biological descendant.

The Bible and Koran lay down rules which, 1,500 or even 3,000 years ago may have been an improvement on the customs of surrounding tribes but today, in the twenty-first century in a globalised world, are simply abuses of human rights on a grand scale. The evil is multiplied when reinterpretation of such scripture is forbidden. Only in a portion of the globe and very recently has there been a significant breakthrough on this front in the ongoing battle for freedom of the human spirit and even this may not be permanent.

The monarchy in the UK is a highly sophisticated exploitation of institutional religion. The establishment very cleverly effects the interpenetration of religion and state power by implying a sort of quasi-divine status for the monarch while simultaneously projecting a picture of 'ordinariness'. Their lives are a living fairy tale, part of the so-called celebrity culture yet at the same time they are 'just like us'. Which means there has to be a changing picture of the royal family if social control is to be maintained, as the British establishment is astute enough to realise.

Royal families and other establishment figures such as presidents are all supposed to reflect the current morality and to pay homage to established religions as part of their routine. Backsliding may be frowned upon (Bill Clinton, Edward VIII, for example) but it need not be a disaster (Princess Margaret) and the established church is always at hand to emphasise the necessity for its particular morality to be the foundation for everyone's personal life, whoever they are.

The claim is open and explicit that only religion can

be the basis for morality. However, you only have to take a few examples of good and evil deeds to see that this claim has no foundation. Good deeds have been done by the religious and the secular (Martin Luther King on one hand and Nelson Mandela on the other). Evil, similarly, has been perpetrated by the religious and the secular (Torquemada and Pol Pot). As far as individuals are concerned, there is no correlation between good and evil on one hand and religious and secular on the other. Socially, at the institutional level, it hardly needs to be said that religion has been the cause of much suffering whatever the professed doctrines were and whatever the comfort that has been brought to the adherents.

In fact, since the nineteenth century sociobiological research has provided more and more evidence that morality has its roots in animal group living as it helps the group to flourish. Natural selection would surely favour a morality assisting group survival and altruism would eventually be a natural outcome of such a morality? And it has not stopped at this. Humanity has gone far beyond the biological roots of altruism into paths of love, compassion, opposition to injustice and emotions of even greater complexity. As Richard Dawkins has written, humanity has transcended its DNA and may act in such a way as would make its DNA think it was mad.

It is around the issue of morality that the human spirit has one of its hardest struggles for freedom. Religious institutions take the heartfelt yearnings of individual people to lead a good life and impose rules and regulations which force them into living as human beings were never intended and which are a major cause of unhappiness for millions. And even if the unhappiness can be moderated by adjustment, untold numbers are cut off from the fulfilment that is their birthright. Rules and regulations governing sexual behaviour are at the centre of such distortions including, of course, laws about whom we are allowed to love.

In case the picture has strayed too far in the direction of pessimism, it must be said that all is not lost. How could it be since actual progress has been achieved in so many fields in recent years? For, although it may seem that powerful establishments, both religious and secular, reign supreme and have all the important forces at their disposal, it remains the case that in every human being a spark is always kept safe and sound and free right at the centre of one's being even though it is not acknowledged socially or communicated. This spark might be called 'the soul' even though this word has religious connotations. It is the hidden part of the human spirit, the very private part which is cherished and kept alive but is not usually displayed.

When an artist paints a picture and does so by assembling the elements of his/her milieu and reassembling them, what is added in so doing comes from the 'soul' of the artist. The 'wholeness' of the picture is over-and-above the simple sum of the elements going into it. It is instantly recognisable but no words are adequate to describe it or its effects and impact. It is this soul that we have to be grateful to for human progress although even this has been hijacked by the religious establishment. Mind, consciousness, the human spirit and its essence or soul are all emergent properties of the material world organised in a special way. Religious doctrine would have us believe that the soul is an entity separate from the body and put there by a transcendental deity. We are threatened with losing this deeply cherished aspect of our selves if we transgress or break the chains that tie us to what is socially demanded of us in the rules and regulations. People like ourselves were burned alive for believing in a particular religious doctrine and the justification was that it would save their souls.

Beliefs and Needs

Even those of us who pride ourselves on our rationality still have a big problem with the contradiction between the rational and emotional sides of our human nature. And this can manifest itself in many ways, some of which are quite unexpected. For example, Christmas. The idea of the creator of the universe being incarnated into the world as a tiny, helpless baby is an idea of unbelievable beauty. But never forget that it is the *idea* that inspires the emotion, not reality. And the idea that, whatever the problems and suffering any of us may have in this world, there is always an all-powerful deity at hand to be on our side and to give comfort (and joy at Christmas) could not be more reassuring. It must be really comforting to believe that there is a source of unconditional love somewhere who is, simultaneously all-powerful. The problem is the fact that, despite prayers to him on so many occasions, there is relatively rarely a response.

How do so many people keep believing that 'God will provide' when they and their children go hungry day after day? Answers to prayers, like miraculous occurrences, seem to occur very selectively.

Such faith must make what seem to be unbearably hard lives bearable. There will be 'pie in the sky when you die by and by', as the old US trade union song had it. I remember saying to a Nigerian friend many years ago that it was not only people in the colonies who struggled – the working class in Britain struggled too. He replied: 'Yes, the British workers struggle to live – the Nigerian workers struggle just not to die.' The life-force must be much more powerful than we think. And all this religiosity works hard to reinforce the social control of the establishment everywhere. Why else would they always be supported by establishments in all but avowedly secular states? (And these have their own form of religion which substitutes for the old-fashioned kind). Religions speak to most people's passionate yearnings – they bring comfort and joy – at a terrible price, however. The price is one's spiritual freedom and, in the final analysis, one's soul.

Another human need calls for attention and that is the love of humanity for stories that apparently give meaning to life. It is highly probable that this need is actually wired into us. Certainly, the mythology of our childhood is an intrinsic part of us even after it seems as if it has been rejected by our rational, cognitive selves – it remains as the mythology which was once believed in.

In the Soviet Union and other similar countries there

was a mythology resembling religion. This is hardly surprising because the 'story' told by Marx closely resembled a religious one of achieving a heaven (communist society) starting from a state of sinfulness (capitalist society). Communism was the Kingdom of Heaven and the proletariat represented the saints. The inadequacy of this particular mythology was revealed after the fall of most of these countries when old people were found to have kept to the ancient beliefs of the church and many young people soon embraced these superstitions. However, despite this, the likeness of the myth to a religious one does not invalidate Marx's basic concepts and humanity's need for a society a lot better than the one we now have all over the globe. Nor does it invalidate his unsurpassed analysis of the capitalist system.

Even before this, Marx had developed a model in which history is a battle between labour and capital. He and Engels began *The Communist Manifesto* with the words, 'The history of all hitherto existing society is the history of class struggles.' According to Marx, man has been alienated from his true self by class society and by the necessity to spend one's life producing commodities which will be wrested from him. Only the revolution, resulting first in socialism and then, after the right conditions have been put in place, communism, its full fruition, will restore his true self.

The religious essence of Marxism was obscured by Marx's opposition to religion but it was certainly moralistic in that capitalism was implicitly evil in its effects in expropriating the product of the labour of the proletariat. Socialism and communism certainly represented 'good' societies.

Christianity and Marxism may be put into two columns:

CHRISTIANITY	MARXISM
God	Stalin, Mao, etc.
Salvation of the soul	Slavery to freedom Reclamation of self from alienation
Redemption by Day of Judgement	Proletarian revolution
Unity of theory and practice	Unity of theory and practice
Salvation by works or faith	Salvation by revolutionary action
Saints and angels	Proletariat
Kingdom of Heaven	Communist society
Christian community	Communist Party
Bible	Marxist theory
Inevitability	Inevitability

In his book *Myth and Ritual in Christianity*, p.7, Alan Watts defines myth as '...a complex of stories - some no doubt fact, and some phantasy - which, for various reasons, human beings regard as demonstrations of the inner meaning of the universe and of human life.' Myth, as he writes, is concrete and vivid, and may consist of narratives, images, rites, ceremonies or symbols. Why do some legends acquire the status of myth? It seems to have something to do with embodying the 'world-feeling' of millions.

Clinging to myth as if it were historical fact may not destroy its power over many people, and so it ossifies into being idolatrous. Stories become 'set in stone'. They become dead idols. They should be creative images. If other people's stories do not suit us but we need something like them, we are actually free to make up our own stories which do suit us. And these may be about such eschatological phenomena as life and death, beginnings and ends. The necessary condition for this to be healthy is that we remember that these stories are made up for our own personal use and we do not allow them to render us helpless or subservient in any way to any person or collection of people.

The stories about Jesus of Nazareth and his life and death have been turned into such idolatrous narratives, used to impose social control. The transformation of Jesus of Nazareth into Jesus Christ permitted the committing of dreadful atrocities by the Church set up in his name. Jesus was presented as alienated from his

Jewish co-religionists and countrymen and, simultaneously, as their victim. 'The Jews killed Christ' was used for two thousand years as the basis for anti-semitism when the ruling elite wanted a scapegoat for their own class oppression of ordinary people. To add insult to injury, Jesus is presented in the Gospels as deeply antagonistic to his own people (For example, John 8:31ff.).

This does not have to be the case though. Surely it is obvious that some of the Bible can be treated just like other literature and the sheer poetry of its language may be savoured and enjoyed like any other literature? We experience no problem with our response to the poetry of Shakespeare. The Bible should take its proper place as legendary literature in the culture of mankind.

People often express awareness of the transcendent through symbolism and, therefore, through some form of myth. Symbolism presents what is non-visualisable in a form which is visualisable. But a *God* conceptually defined in words by means of myth necessarily becomes an idol except to the most devout and highly conscientious mystics. This is inevitable, however much believers may hate the idea. It is inevitable because words are symbols and to think in terms of them as reality is a form of image-making and therefore of idol-worship. The most that words can do is to point to the truth. Belief is the opposite of faith which is open to the Suchness.

Unfortunately, no one encourages us to make up our own stories, those which would suit our own particular needs and special circumstances. I have more than one story of this kind which keeps me from missing my late loved ones too much and they give me considerable consolation. But they are my myths, my stories, and I know that they are not really 'truth'. (Although they may be, in a sense, during the time I tell them to myself). Because I know that I am dealing in myth, in symbolism, such stories are never totally satisfactory but at any particular moment they simultaneously do and do not satisfy my hunger for consolation. This is the best I can do. And I do not sell my freedom, integrity or self-dependence in so doing. In this process the constant movement of our consciousness guarantees that we both search and find all the time. As a matter of fact, we all construct forms of myth in the course of our lives with respect to all sorts of worldly aspects of our lives but with the knowledge (if we are sane) that these are fantasies so there is usually nothing to be afraid of.

A genuinely satisfactory myth cannot be constructed artificially, it has to grow organically. You have to be 'open' to the cosmos if something fruitful is to form in your consciousness. I am talking here not of socially-evolved mythology but of personally-emergent stories , making sense of things. And you have to depend on your capacity to think in an *as if* way. The last is more significant than appears. It means that one is able to experience comfort from something that one has constructed *as if* it were the truth while, at the same time, knowing that it is not. It is just like the way we treat numerals *as if* they were numbers whilst knowing full well that they are merely symbols for these.

It is also necessary to realise that your myth may not suit anybody else. Other people's myths may 'turn you on' and that is all right provided that you retain the knowledge of their mythic character and do not allow them to rule your behaviour and thought.

We should not fall into the trap of assuming (as we are urged to by outside authorities) that the best things in our lives are provided from the outside by a transcendental being. We all know very well how much we depend on music for immense spiritual joy and to this must be added the joy from painting, poetry, drama, dance, stories, novels, the wonders of nature and so on – one could go on for a long time. And we must add the (very probably) greater joy of creation in these very spheres. There can be no doubt that any form of creativity in these arts is the very essence of spiritual activity.

The universe has, via the channel of human beings, created all this for us and many of us think we could not live without these sources of ecstasy in our lives. When I listen to music such as the *St Matthew* or the *St John Passion,* I thank the universe for creating it. The universe is amply capable of creating such sublime music via Johann Sebastian Bach. There is no need of an outside agent to do it.

Why, looking at a beautiful cathedral, do I feel so marvellous, when I am a nontheist? Whoever built or designed it must have had deep religious feelings and probably wanted to 'glorify God'. The design normally indicates that they wanted to reach out for something nobler than themselves. They surely had comparable emotions to mine when I look at it. The builders saw themselves as reaching towards God – I do not share that in its particularity but I share the emotions. Who is to say that their feelings were deeper than mine?

On surveying that which I am and what is around me I cannot see or experience in any way whatsoever, spiritual or otherwise, any sort of external deity or feel any sort of external presence. By external I mean external to the universe itself. Anything I experience seems very much a part of the universe. And I cannot join the medievals in attributing transcendence as well as immanence to a being simply in order to render possible its existence. For me, there is nothing there. I do not know what others experience nor do I know how justified their interpretations are of their experiences. I cannot know.

It is , therefore, impossible for me to accept any form of theism or God of any sort or any externally-imposed representation of reality. I know that I do not know about the beginning and end of the universe. I know that I shall never have satisfactory answers to the big questions presented earlier in this chapter but, equally, the variety of answers given by the multifarious religions seem less than satisfactory to me. I know that what I think I know is totally inadequate and that I make my own myths. As a nontheist, God is for me a human construct, a (mythical) idea. However, the truly astonishing and wonderful thing is that I am free to fantasise about such a being in any way I please and under any circumstances that arise. Provided, that is, that I do not invest my fantasy with reality.

What is impossible is to put myself into servitude – to exchange my soul's independence and my freedom of thought and action for the false comfort of the myth of an all-powerful, loving parent. That is more suitable for a small child than a mature adult.

The good news emerging from a self-referring universe is that we are on our own, free to think for ourselves, answerable to ourselves for our conclusions and do not have to be bound by old rules or old habits of thought. We are called upon to be grown-up.

W. E. Henley, a Victorian poet of a rather old-fashioned kind, expresses my feelings well:

UNCONQUERABLE

Out of the night that covers me,
Black as the pit from pole to pole,
I thank whatever gods may be
For my unconquerable soul.

In the fell clutch of circumstance
I have not winced nor cried aloud:
Under the bludgeonings of chance
My head is bloody, but unbow'd.

Beyond this place of wrath and tears
Looms but the Horror of the shade,
And yet the menace of the years
Finds and shall find me unafraid.

It matters not how strait the gate,
How charged with punishments the scroll,
I am the master of my fate:
I am the captain of my soul.

Theory of the Nature of God

Unexpected though it may be, we are going to spare a little sympathy for a group of men and women who had serious problems in considering humanity's relationship to the universe in the form of humanity's relationship to its gods, that is, theology. These people were the medieval theologians, some of whom were mystics, whose intelligence and sincerity clashed with their conditioning and must also have clashed with their unwillingness to be sacrificed as living torches on the altars of the power structures of their time.

Christian theologian-mystics (on whom I shall focus), tied themselves in verbal knots in the attempt to reconcile the clarity of their vision of the cosmos with the details of Christian theology and the Trinity in particular. They referred to their God in three ways in order to perform this reconciliation. First, there was the 'Ground of Being', for which I have so far been unable to find a satisfactory meaning (except for 'condition of existence') but it is often used as an alternative to simply 'God' (the second means of reference). Thirdly, there is the 'Godhead', which may refer to the divine nature but is also closely related to God as a Trinity.

It seems that the main problem was to reconcile the unchanging, attributeless nature of their deity with the possibility of change and the possession of attributes in the particular form of the birth of Jesus (considered to be the Son of God and as having the same substance as God). In fact, the problem was the philosophical one of having a divinity which was simultaneously pure Being and yet pure Becoming.

They went on to worry about various problems such as those connected with the Trinity: had it existed for all time? Did Jesus exist before time had been created? Such problems existed in the context of their main goal, which was to attain perfect union with a God who was seen as simultaneously transcendent and immanent. To grasp such a contradiction was highly courageous on their part as well as highly sophisticated.

Jewish mystic theology was and is distinct from the Christian variety. Jewish mysticism has existed since about the second century but came into its own and had its most fertile period at the beginning of the thirteenth century after its centre had moved to Germany and Provence. The principal problem was the reconciliation of the God whose Being was transcendent with the God of the Bible, who was very personal indeed. There was an abyss between these two conceptions which it was the goal of such mystics to cross.

The bridging of the abyss was achieved through a form of symbolism known as the Kabbalah, in which the attributes of God were represented in words on a sort of 'tree of life' and also through numerology (known as Gematria). Jewish mysticism was non-absorptive in the sense that the mystic could not be totally absorbed into the God he/she was seeking and could not have union with but only 'cleave' to that God because God and man have nothing in common. This suggests a similarity to the transcendence and immanence of the Christian God but it differed profoundly from this. The latter involved the simultaneous attribution of transcendence and immanence to God whereas the former had a so-called 'abyss' to overcome. And whereas Christian mystics could be burned for heresy the Jewish mystics could only be excommunicated as the Jewish religious authorities had no state machine at their disposal.

The Muslim mystic theologians, the best-known of whom was Rumi (1207 - 1273), a Persian poet, had no such good fortune and the first Sufi martyr, (Hallaj), was tortured and killed in AD922 for stating, 'I am the Truth', effectively claiming to be identical with God and therefore becoming a heretic. It should be noted that Meister Eckhart (c.1260 - 1327), the great Dominican mystic, died before being convicted for heresy by the Benedictine Inquisition.

Other, much later thinkers, have done much better. It might surprise the reader to see Albert Einstein classified as a mystic but he qualifies as a deeply religious non-believer as he says himself, who was overcome with awe at the essential mystery of the cosmos – his motivation for pursuing the hard work of science, so he said. And he is far from being the only nontheist who has experienced the sense of oneness with the cosmos which accompanies total awareness of its (possibly ultimate) impenetrable mystery.

I wonder what the mystical experiences are like which mystics are supposed to have? I have never been trained in meditation but have done what many books have told me to do. This has been ineffective as I may have felt closer to the universe and very much at peace but have never felt anything so startlingly different from anything else that I would be prepared to say that I have experience of God.

The important thing is that, whether the medieval mystics 'experienced' something divine or not, they left writings behind in which their beliefs were expressed and these writings certainly constitute solid evidence of their rationally expressed thoughts, if nothing else. One of the questions at issue is whether the alleged experiences of the mystics are self-validating or not. There can be no question that they had experiences which took them from the level of the everyday onto something very different. That is not the issue. The issue is the origin of such experiences and it is there that theists and nontheists separate.

Many possible material explanations exist for experiences which seem to lift the subject into a state of exaltation and these range from chemical secretions in the brain through epilepsy to the postulation of other dimensions into which it is possible to be transported. There is no doubt, though, that there have been, throughout the ages, a number of people called 'mystics' who have or have not had a variety of experiences which have enabled them to have, in some cases, highly enlightening insights about the cosmos.

There is a wide variation between the Christian

mystics and there are some (possibly the majority) with whom any nontheist would feel no sense of rapport at all. Others, however, the ones not consistently repeating the Christian message, seem to be struggling to make sense of their spiritual life in a way that does not tirelessly repeat expressions of adoration of the Trinity. They are clearly in the grip of a quandary about their spiritual life – they are tying themselves in knots in order that their intellectual, spiritual and conventionally religious views are not hopelessly at variance with one another.

Their spiritual and intellectual problems arose following the transformation of Jesus of Nazareth into the Jesus Christ of the Roman Catholic Church. By the time of Meister Eckhart, at the end of the thirteenth and beginning of the fourteenth century, there was a lot of theological undergrowth to plough through in order to reach their God. They had to find some way of accounting for an unchanging God of eternity who, simultaneously, was actually born into this world of time. And there were problems connected with the Trinity such as: Had it existed for all time? Did Jesus, whose substance was the same as that of God, exist before the creation of time?

Their problem was that they were thinking people, highly intelligent and with a high level of intellectual honesty. They were widely read and familiar with theology and philosophy and were capable of putting two and two together. I refer here to the medievals, particularly Meister Eckhart, as I have not yet found another to equal him, certainly not more recent writers.

What surely must have been a major problem is the reconciliation of Being with Becoming (in the putative deity). That is, how to reconcile a timeless, eternal Creator with the God with whom Jesus was supposed to share identical substance? The latter form of God was one capable of differentiation, he was not a simple one, nameless, Absolute, and he was certainly not timeless as an important aspect of him existed in time in the form of Jesus.

And then there was the fact that God had to be simultaneously transcendent and immanent. For a theist, this simultaneity must have been an exalting thought. But it must have taken a great deal of courage to maintain both properties simultaneously in the face of their contradictory character. Yet both attributes had to appertain to God. You do not have to be a theist to appreciate the immensity of the achievement of these medievals in grasping the contradiction. The next step is the realisation that such a situation corresponds to our own experience when we listen to the music of J. S. Bach – it appears to be simultaneously transcendent and immanent.

A third problem inherent in the theology of the medieval church was that of reconciling a God thought to be empty of attributes with the notion of a God thought to have an infinity of attributes. The emptiness notion springs from the idea of a God with nothing in common with the material world. The infinitude of God gives birth to the idea of a God with an infinite number of attributes.

It is Meister Eckhart (c.1260 – c.1327, German) who

provides, in his paradoxes, the most wonderful vision of what a God would be if such a being existed. This, of course, is Meister Eckhart's vision.

'The Godhead is as void as though it were not.' (Qu. Aldous Huxley, *The Perennial Philosophy*, p.25). In other words, the Godhead is as free of attributes (properties) as though it did not exist.

'The more God is in all things, the more He is outside them. The more He is without, the more within.' (Meister Eckhart, Qu. Huxley, p.2).

'Why dost thou prate of God? Whatever thou sayest of Him is untrue.' (Meister Eckhart, Qu. Huxley, p.125). There are no words to express anything about God, and certainly not one's thoughts about him. So we had better stop even thinking about such a concept. And as finite beings we can intuit nothing about him. Thus, even if there were a being with the name God, it would be impossible to know or say anything about him whatsoever.

'The eye through which I see God is the same eye as that through which God sees me.' (Meister Eckhart, *Sermons*). This saying becomes clear only when one substitutes 'universe' for 'God'. When I did this I saw that it was saying the same thing as I would say. If I (as part of the universe) look at a friend (another part of the universe) and vice versa, then we see the same light in each other by means of the same light. (See above, Chapter 2, pp.25-26).

'Thou must love God as not-God, not-Spirit, not-person, not-image, but as He is, a sheer, pure absolute One, sundered from all two-ness, and in whom we must eternally sink from nothingness to nothingness.' (Meister Ekhart, Qu. Huxley, p.32).

This last idea, that of nothingness, is itself an abstraction. And, as in any other abstraction, it *represents* the reality of nothingness. Which leaves Meister Eckhart as a nontheist, surely? If, however, Meister Eckhart is referring to nothingness as an abstraction, then his God is a double abstraction. However, so much of his writing is definitely Christian that one is forced to conclude that he is not a nontheist but is in the 'grey area' of what one might call 'Is-Isnotness'.

Perhaps this is Meister Eckhart's way of nontheism. He had reached the limits of possible expression of thought. He abolished all representation/symbolism and saw there was nothing to be said. To say anything must be idolatrous. But he could not let go so he expressed his most basic beliefs as paradoxes! Since God has not finally been abandoned by Meister Eckhart, he has to behave *as if* God might exist through his expression in terms of paradox. The paradoxes refer to the extraordinary attribute of God – his *as ifness.*

Meister Eckhart must have been struggling with his belief system as most of his writing is devotedly theistic and Christian. Perhaps the truth is that there was a conflict between his reason and his emotion.

His writing was actually not always as straightforward as it seemed and he saw far more as symbolism than was customary in his time. For example, in his Sermon 25 (Selected Writings, Penguin Classics, pp.222), he interprets the story about Jesus' childhood, in which his parents had to return to Jerusalem for him when he was not to be found, as the need to return to the source and ground from which you came and leave the crowd behind.

What did he really believe? He got as close as possible to a statement of nontheism in his paradoxes but it is hard to believe that he really was a nontheist. Added to which, the circumstances under which he lived would have put him in grave danger of a horrendous form of execution had he been branded as an apostate. Meister Eckhart was a Dominican and he was eventually tried by a Benedictine Inquisition on the charge of heresy. He died before being sentenced.

He was a hair's breadth away from denying a Christian God. And it has been said that Buddha himself never mentioned God because people would not understand what he was talking about.

Probably the most likely explanation of the apparent inconsistency of Meister Eckhart is a deep and powerful awareness of the dangers of idolatry. This may extend even to ideas as when we stop being 'open to new light' and our beliefs become ossified. As F. C. Happold writes: 'Dogma is the translation of mystical experience and the insights which spring from it into symbol.' Thus dogmatism and idolatry fuse in the worship of any form of symbolism, whether it be an idol, a mental picture, a frozen set of words in a book written hundreds of years ago or any set of beliefs, even one's own as if they were 'set in stone'.

Why is idolatry so repellent? It is the worship of the symbol instead of the reality. It involves an inferior substitute to give spurious meaning to life. It means demeaning yourself! It means taking the inferior symbol for the sake of an immediate inferior benefit.

In any belief system, if one goes to extremes in order to avoid idolatry then it is possible to lose any sense of the sacred. This results from over-anxiety that attachment to any belief system may be overdone and may become itself a form of idolatry. (It may be understood that 'idolatry' and 'sacred' may both be used in a religious and a non-religious sense). So, the problem is that of reconciling the avoidance of idolatry with retaining some sense of the sacredness of certain values or principles. Just as we wish not to be rigid, we are aware of the danger of too great flexibility. There have to be principles and there has to be a degree of stability but, on the other hand, we wish to be 'open to new light'.

Modern theists have to take the present state of science into account and do so with apparent ease but then, instead of justifying their theistic belief system, they make the illogical leap into theism and religion. It might be said that theists today justify their God and religion by predominantly appealing to emotion but violating logic. Nontheists, on the other hand, are supremely logical but in their writings sometimes tend to underestimate emotion.

Not so for Meister Eckhart. He courageously faced the problematic (?) spiritual situation he found himself in and presented it to us. His idea of God , when taken to its boundaries, implied the most thrilling and exhilarating paradoxes. And he certainly took things to the boundaries of existence, which is where we know we are when we are in the realm of paradox. This is so because it is only in the 'grey area' between two zones of existence that the only form of expression is by means of paradox. Although he expressed this in theistic terms, he took us to the boundaries of human thought in relation to the cosmos and our place in it.

CHAPTER 4

Mathematics and the Human Spirit

Up to this point, the subject matter of this book has been to do principally with religion and the idea of God. Have we now departed from this? No, we have not, as the Prologue and Introduction explained. We are still pursuing the same objectives which are to show, first, what extraordinary delight and feelings of awe and reverence may be obtained from all sorts of aspects of the universe which (to the ordinary reader) might seem to have little if anything to do with religion; secondly, to point out the miracles of creativity which humanity itself has achieved and all with no need of a transcendental deity. This is what I hope to convey in this chapter in relation to mathematics.

For the mathematician, mathematics is a supremely satisfying intellectual and aesthetic experience. And yet it is not an easy field to work in – ask any working mathematician and she/he will agree that mathematics is *hard*. But it is marvellous, nevertheless.

What other field do we all operate in during most of our ordinary lives all the time, yet most of us have never passed an examination in mathematics? In order to survive we have to be able to estimate distances, directions, times and forces. We need to convey the food from the plate to our mouths. We need to estimate the time from home to the station. We need to estimate the right pressure to put on the door handle to push it open.

It is a commonplace that mathematics is essential for the existence of the modern world. However, the bonus for anyone studying it to any depth at all (even the relatively simple level of a first degree) is its utter beauty of form and symmetry. Every civilization has created some mathematics in order to survive and, more important, to develop in every way. And we human beings did it ourselves.

There are no actual numbers (as distinct from signs for them) floating about in the world around us. Number is an abstraction from the material world as it exists and it is people who have constructed the mathematical relationships corresponding to the relationships implicit in the structure of the universe. Where else could mathematics have come from? Only from the self-referring interaction of human beings by means of the perceptive mechanism and the reflective brain, connecting with the universe itself. And it all originated with the experience of the heartbeat and the pulse.

What else but mathematics has its potential relationships embedded in the universe?

What else but mathematics is constructed out of these very relationships?

It is really foolish in the extreme to try to capture in a few pages the miracle of mathematics. What follows is a brief discussion about some aspects of mathematics which I have found particularly satisfying aesthetically.

They all evoke the joy of what I would call 'mathematical spirituality'.

Readers may notice that some expected topics are absent. e.g. Golden Section, Fibonacci Series, Sacred Geometry. These topics, which are particular sooner than general and involve ratios and proportions sooner than numbers, have not been mentioned separately because they have not been, for me, major sources of spiritual excitement.

Proof and Certainty

The certainty of mathematics has been a part of humanity's cultural assumptions for a very long time. And this is not only a question of 1 + 1 = 2, 2 + 2 = 4 and so forth. It was around the third century BC in the Hellenistic world that a sort of 'leap' apparently took place in human thought. At this time the Greek geometer Euclid (c. 300BC) took a lot of previously known geometrical propositions, put them into logical order, stated the axioms upon which this ordering was based (such as that the shortest distance between two points is a straight line) and published a geometry book called *Elements*. This word meant the basic principles of the subject.

Educated people revered this work as a model of mathematical certainty and absolute truth until the end of the eighteenth century (apart from one postulate). It is not surprising that this work was admired so much and for so long, as there are few things so satisfying both aesthetically and intellectually as an economical and watertight proof. Even more exciting, however, is the fact that it turned out that even this paragon of logical rigour should be approached with caution. The logic of Euclid turned out to be no more absolutely valid than the number fact 1 + 1 = 2.

Around the end of the eighteenth century, in the tumultuous times heralding the French Revolution, there were mathematicians who queried the very axioms upon which apparent mathematical certainty was based. What if these axioms/premises were not the case? What happens if we make other suppositions? Suppose that parallel lines do not meet at infinity? The result was the construction of new geometries which turned out to be applicable to spaces different from the everyday one we inhabit. For example, a geometry was invented which turned out later to correspond to the curved space of Einstein's general relativity and not our own familiar space of straight lines. The absoluteness of mathematics turned out to be relative, that is, conditional. The geometry you arrive at depends on the assumptions you lay down at the start. This holds for any logical system, not only a mathematical one. You have to lay down in advance the rules that it will have to follow and you start from those. Then you see what this leads to. However, once the axioms are set out and the logic pursued on the basis of these axioms, the resulting system is certain. (But only in our universe.)

Similarly, if the substantive base for 1 + 1 = 2 alters, for example if we are referring to raindrops and not individual solid things, then the arithmetic will be different. 1 raindrop meeting 1 raindrop on a window pane may well result in 1 raindrop when they merge and not two raindrops. So both situations have relative, and not absolute, logics.

Nevertheless, even when this is taken into account, the power of the logic of mathematics is awe-inspiring. In fact, the logic is even more powerful because we understand the necessity of taking into consideration the conditions under which we are working. Moreover, we now know that we are free to lay down any axioms we want and to let the logic lead us where it must go. Just make sure that you make the right assumptions before you make logical deductions. Having done so, an apparently watertight proof in mathematics gives a sense of aesthetic completeness unlike anything else.

Symbolism

The second and, perhaps, even more impressive feature of the power of mathematics is its symbolic character. This may appear obvious, especially if you are accustomed to algebra. But most people are not so accustomed. And the reason that people find mathematics hard is that it is abstract. And the reason that mathematics performs its tasks so well is precisely because it is so abstract.

A true mathematical symbolism is one that has abstracted only the quantitative aspect from what it represents and has none of its vivid, concrete qualities. Moreover, it is totally detached from what it represents and exists at a different level. Thus, if there are three cups , the numeral used to represent the number of cups, '3', has nothing in this sign which corresponds in any way to the nature of the cups, their colour, shape or any other property. Mathematics is concerned with quantity (that is, number or amount) and is indifferent to the qualities of things.

At a simple level, if we are adding whole things, we are not tied to cups but, as we all know, the numerals may refer to any things whatsoever. So even a simple numeral system opens the door to unlimited possibilities.

Thus, the invention of even the simplest numeral system is a sort of miracle, where the word 'miracle' is used in the broadest sense and is not restricted to religion.

The Definition of Number

We are going on to look at this definition, not because it is a particular cause of excitement in itself but because it has something in common with the abstract definition of God which human beings have recently constructed. This definition is not easy to understand and must be taken step-by-step. It was first put forward by Gottlob Frege (1848 – 1925) in 1884 in a rather more difficult form and later followed up by Bertrand Russell (1872 – 1970).

First, think of a set of three cups. Then try and think of all the sets of three things you could possibly have which correspond numerically to this set (for the mathematical reader this means being in one-to-one correspondence to the original set of three cups). This is the (big) set consisting of all (small) sets of three things that are, ever have been or ever will be, in the universe. (This is a thought experiment only). Then abstract the 'threeness' from each of these (small) sets of three things. Then, taking all these 'threenesses' together, abstract the 'threeness' that they all have in common, and you are left with a totally abstract 'threeness' (without any vestiges of the qualities of the things involved).

The number 'three' symbolised by '3' is this last 'threeness'. It is an abstraction from an abstraction from the (concrete) original three cups. It is a double abstraction and corresponds to the concept of God as a double abstraction.

Hindu – Arabic Numerals

In introducing the idea of mathematical symbolism, the example used was a familiar one from our own, traditional Hindu – Arabic system. These numeral signs were brought to Europe by an Arab mathematician called Al-Khowarizmi (or Al-Khwarizmi) (died c.825) but were actually invented in India in the sixth century AD. Ordinary though they are, and obvious though they may seem, they have characteristics which have made them especially productive and creative over the years.

On the practical side, when they arrived in Western Europe they were superbly suited to the new, burgeoning capitalist system, still in its infancy, but nevertheless already putting down its roots in Northern Italy. Capitalism was always a credit economy and the possibility of using the new numerals for trading purposes meant that they were very soon used by the merchants of the time. You could not keep long-term records on an abacus but these numerals were very suited to double-entry bookkeeping. That meant that records of debits and credits could be kept using them.

However, it is their theoretical features which are more significant in the present context. As we all know, the system consists of ten numerals (including zero), and it is what is known as a place-value notation. That is, the value of a digit depends upon its place, the column it is in. '23' is a totally different number from '32'. It certainly satisfies all the conditions for a true mathematical symbolism as it is a quantitative abstraction and detached from any concrete things it refers to. It can be used in an unlimited number of situations.

These ten signs are infinitely interchangeable and their use may be compared with writing a symphony with the limited number of notes available to the composer. They can be extended infinitely to the left or the right to show very large or very small numbers. You can use a decimal point to separate whole numbers on the left from fractions to the right of it and this decimal point may be moved to the right or the left. Such movement shows the relativity (conditionality) of the numerical unit which reflects the relativity of wholes and parts in the physical universe. In other words the numeral sign '1' may refer both to a whole and to a part of a whole. You can calculate with decimals as if they were whole numbers and this was a great recommendation when they were presented to the world in 1585 in a book by Simon Stevin (1548 – 1620).

Although the Hindu-Arabic numerals are only signs for numbers, we (rightly) treat them 'as if' they were the numbers themselves. It is this 'as-ifness' which is so useful and important. These numerals have performed sterling service over the years and still do, although so much more mathematics has been invented since the numerals were first invented in sixth century India.

New Numbers from Old

Starting with the natural numbers 1, 2, 3, ... everything else followed over historical time. New mathematical entities were constructed; fractions, negative numbers (-1, -2, -3,..); irrational numbers (square root of 2, square root of 3,...) and imaginary numbers (those involving square root of -1). All except fractions were initially deemed false or impossible, to be rejected until practical necessity and developments in mathematics forced upon mathematicians the recognition and acceptance of these numbers and their incorporation into the corpus of mathematics. Even fractions were not admitted to be numbers by the ancient Egyptians who treated them as (smaller) whole numbers and had enormously complicated ways of calculating with them.

Is it any wonder that non-mathematicians find mathematics difficult when it involves dealing with such extraordinary things as negative numbers? Don't even mention imaginary numbers. There is a rumour that a member of the Pythagorean School was thrown off a cliff for telling non-members that numbers (called irrational) existed which could not be divided into an exact number of units!

There are other numbers, special constants of nature (represented by letters), which constantly emerge together in mathematics in the same expressions but have totally different origins. For example, e relates to growth in a wide variety of different fields, and i, which turns out to be involved in the solutions of some equations and has applications in electromagnetism and subatomic physics. Mathematics demonstrates as nothing else, perhaps, the interconnectedness inherent in the universe.

Algebraic Symbolism

The algebra first appearing in Europe, which had originated in India and had been added to and transmitted by the Arab mathematicians, was written in words and not in symbols. From about the thirteenth century onwards different abbreviations were used for algebraic quantities in different European countries and what finally emerged in 1637 (in Descartes' *La Géométrie*) was what we are familiar with from our schooldays.

The symbolism which was ready just when it was needed, in the seventeenth century, was not only magnificently suited to expressing scientific laws but, because it was fully cipherised and separate from its substantive base, it could be totally indifferent to the actual content of that base. Its special magic is that it is applicable to an unlimited number of different situations and is indifferent to what it represents. x may stand for anything – a number of sheep, the length of a carpet, the height of a mountain, anything you please. You can form an equation which corresponds to the situation in which you are interested and solve the problem about sheep or carpets or mountains.

Our traditional algebra is the generalisation of ordinary numbers. But we are not restricted to this. We can invent any algebraic system we like, based on any premises (axioms) we care to lay down. For example, we are used to the commutative law for numbers ($3 \times 2 = 2 \times 3$ for example). This is true for all ordinary numbers but it doesn't have to be so. We are free to construct a different system by laying down different rules. For example we might say: let $a \times b = - b \times a$. We can then carry on and see what happens. It is a 'what if?' situation.

Mathematicians started to do such things in the nineteenth century with fruitful results. New systems emerged corresponding to new elements and operations and were found to correspond to new situations. The new rule I suggested above belongs to an algebra corresponding to the subatomic level.

Infinity

Two concepts have captured the imagination even of non-mathematicians over the centuries, both of which seem to take us into the zone of existence which is non-material and especially pertains to the human spirit. These concepts are infinity and zero.

Infinity has been an object of awe, puzzlement and paradox for centuries. In fact, mathematicians and philosophers have had differing ideas about the nature of the infinite, sometimes taking the view (with some degree of plausibility) that it cannot exist. Aristotle thought you could only have a potential infinity and there is a great deal to be said for this viewpoint. We live in a finite world - no matter how far you travel you are still in a particular, finite place. It is not possible to experience infinity. It is a mathematical idea. And it can surely only come from the possibility of minds forming questions like: 'What if—?' What would happen if you went on and on and never stopped?

Look at the natural numbers 1, 2, 3,... What is the last one? Is there a last one? If not, then the idea of infinity follows and is progressively perfected in the course of mathematical history. Extraordinary though it may seem, the great philosopher G. F. W. Hegel (1770-1831) wrote that infinity is that which has no beginning and no end and the only entity fulfilling these conditions is the circle!

As a matter of fact, Galileo (1564 - 1642) argued that there could be no such thing as infinity because, if there were, then for the series of whole numbers, the whole would be equal to a part of itself. Why did he argue like this

Consider the natural numbers 1, 2, 3, 4, ...

Take a part of this series, the even numbers: 2, 4, 6, 8, ...

You can take each of these one by one from each line and pair them off with each other (that is, 1 with 2; 2 with 4; 3 with 6 and so on) and never reach the end. You will never be short of an even number to pair off with a number in the top line. So, if there were infinitely many natural numbers, you could pair them off with the evens (a part of the series of natural numbers). This would mean the whole would equal to a part of itself and so, Galileo argued, infinity cannot exist. Notice that, if the number of whole numbers were finite, you would run out of evens to pair them off with.

It was not until the second half of the nineteenth century that serious progress was made by Georg Cantor (1845 – 1918) who had the courage to grasp the contradiction by asserting that the very definition of an infinite series was that it could be put into one-to-one correspondence with a part (subset) of itself. Cantor put this before the mathematical community but it was not well-received at the time and poor Georg Cantor had more than one nervous breakdown as a result.

Amazingly, from this it can be shown that the infinity of mathematical points on a small section of a straight line can be put into one-to-one correspondence with all the mathematical points in infinite, three-dimensional space. If this seems absurd, remember that we are dealing with infinity, which has a strange algebra of its own (e.g. infinity plus infinity = infinity). Viewed cosmologically, it might be that in constructing the concept of infinity, the universe is trying to reach beyond itself.

Zero

Another wonderful mathematical idea is zero. How clever of mathematicians to take the concept of nothing/nothingness and transform it into a mathematical entity – a sign which first stood for 'no sign in this place'. In another context it is a number that may be used to calculate with; in algebra, either a sign for the special element in a system that may be added without altering that upon which it operates or, if we are talking of multiplication, when any element is multiplied by it, it absorbs that element and the answer is zero. [Do not worry if you do not understand all that.]

Zero is now one of the set of whole numbers but this was not always the case. At first, it was only a little 'blob' that was put in the column which had no number in it. By the time it had been transmitted to Europe by the Arab mathematicians it had become a little circle but was still only a place holder and was not always used. There are manuscripts in being in which it appears in some numbers but not in others.

This was still the case in Europe, where it was still not regarded as a number in its own right. The Church condemned the sign together with all other numeral signs as the work of the devil and forbade their use. However, as one might expect, they so facilitated the operations of merchant capital that they were soon extensively used and in this situation, the Church was rendered impotent.

The little circle was not always used at first in arithmetic books and was not standardised until the seventeenth century. Early arithmetic books often omitted zeros from numbers, put every digit in its correct column and, presumably, hoped for the best. (The ancient Babylonians, whose mathematics went back to at least 2,000BC, did not have a sign as a place-filler until about the first century BC). Of course, earlier mathematicians knew that if you add nothing to 6 then the answer is 6. But this is not at all the same thing as thinking of the sign that represented the number zero as an actual numeral exactly like all the others and zero as a number like the others and subject to be used in calculations.

One of the first (if not the very first) mathematicians to use a circle to represent zero – a calculable number – was Thomas Harriot (c.1560 – 1621). This is done in his manuscripts. Isaac Newton (1642 – 1727) lists the natural numbers beginning with 0 in his *Arithmetica Universalis.* As late as 1685, a very distinguished mathematician called John Wallis (1616 – 1703) argued in his *Algebra* that the Greeks had been right in regarding nought as not being a number (but had been wrong in thinking the same of unity). Thereafter, zero had a dignified career, especially in abstract algebra, where it is generalised into what was known as an identity element. (Non-mathematicians, do not worry.) Later, in the twentieth century, Brian Rotman (in *Signifying Nothing: the Semiotics of Zero*, pp.1-6) brilliantly analysed it as a 'meta-sign', a sign about signs which collapsed into a number. Hence, it does not simply stand for nothing at all in the simple sense.

After it achieved the status of a number among other numbers it performed sterling service in completing what is known as the 'real number line'. Without zero, there would by a hiatus/gap between the positive and negative numbers. Had this been the case, he modern world would never have taken off.

Zero has a long and extraordinary history, which is not surprising considering its nature and what it represents. At one time it was a really frightening idea and the Church associated it with the devil in the medieval world.

Reminding ourselves of the creativity of mathematicians, we can still stand amazed at the phenomenon of nothingness/nought/nothing/the void/ emptiness and so on, as necessary conditions for the creation of 'something (zero) out of nothing'. Perhaps, in creating zero, the universe is reaching out for its other?

The Reality of Mathematical Entities

Are mathematical entities real? If so, in what sense? Most readers will think of 1, 2, 3, 4, 5 as numbers but they are not. They are the symbols for numbers but we learn as children to calculate with them *as if* they were numbers themselves. There are no numbers at all in the external world and so we have to invent symbols to represent them.

Numbers are ideas/concepts and if ideas are real, then numbers are real. We do not imagine them. In fact, a so-called imaginary number in mathematics is no more or less imaginary than a 'real' number. We do not think of negative numbers as 'imaginary', just because there are no

'-3 things' in the world around us; we know that negative numbers can be used in real situations such as debts or temperatures just like ordinary whole numbers. Similarly, what are called imaginary numbers in mathematics are applicable to real situations such as electromagnetism and at the quantum level. And imaginary numbers may be the solutions of equations with real coefficients. [Again, do not worry if you do not understand that sentence.]

The Distinguishing Features of Mathematics

What are the characteristics of mathematics which particularly endear it to mathematicians?

First, its universality. Everything in the material world has a quantitative aspect which may be abstracted so that equations may be formed, the solution of which provide the solutions of the problem in hand.

Then the sheer beauty of it. The symmetry of its expressions, the sheer line and form of a well-formed and simple proof-structure (rather like a beautiful sculpture) are truly engaging to the aesthetic sense. What is surprising is that this special form of beauty exists in that which is left *after* the vivid, qualitative features have been abstracted from a situation. This is what draws on our mathematical spirituality.

The unity of mathematics is reassuring and satisfying. Using different methods and different entities we get the same results.

Objectivity is also a feature but only in the sense that nature has the potentiality for mathematical relationships independently of consciousness. The form of expression of these relationships is culturally, socially and individually determined.

We will look at one more twentieth century development in the field of mathematics and briefly mention metamathematics. In metamathematics we reflect upon mathematics instead of actually doing it. A possible task might be to find if a certain proposition is provable or not. Sometimes a bright idea is hit upon but it is not known if it is provable or not. Sometimes it is not, and it is the job of metamathematics to find what is the case and to prove what this has turned out to be. A considerable arsenal of logic of a higher kind than usual is available for metamathematics. Here is the ultimate in self-reference - mathematics referring to itself.

This has been an extremely brief skim over some basic issues and features of mathematics and it is enough to see how the absoluteness of mathematics differs from the absoluteness of religion. In mathematics, you are free at any time to change the axioms and to see what happens, where you are led. This is the polar opposite of religion.

The magic of mathematics resides in the creation out of nothing, by human beings, of a system of thought able to change the world. How does it all work out so well? How does everything 'fit' so perfectly? Perhaps there is a deeper level than we are aware of in the cosmos which determines all this. I do not know. And if any reader does not like questions being posed without the ability to provide answers, one can only say that the human spirit rejoices in the reflections which grapple with such problems.

CHAPTER 5

Science and the Human Spirit

It is not surprising to have a chapter on science in a book discussing nontheism. What may be surprising is that the branch of science under discussion is not biology (especially evolutionary biology) but cosmology and physics, especially their histories. The topics have fired my imagination for most of my life, as I described in the Prologue and Introduction. They are a source of the scientific spirituality which has enthralled me.

This is another chapter in which it is necessary to tax the reader's patience and include a lot of 'facts'. Without these, it would not be possible to convey the full significance of such things as scientific method. Nor would it be possible to convey the transformative effect of the scientific revolution of the seventeenth century on human consciousness. And relativity and quantum theory require some sort of introduction, however brief, if any idea at all is to be given of their revolutionary character. These are the topics which inspired me when I was about fourteen, particularly relativity and quantum theory and that is why I am writing about them now.

The Miracle of Scientific Method

At this point the reader might think that the present chapter will consist of unqualified praise for the truth of scientific facts, the reliability of scientific method and the perfection of scientific theory. This will not be the case. The classical description of scientific method is as follows: The scientist frames a hypothesis, tests it experimentally, performs the experiment, and if the expected result occurs the hypothesis is taken to be correct and is accepted as part of scientific theory. If this does not happen, the hypothesis is rejected.

The experiment should be publicly repeatable and objectively testable. In other words, it should be verifiable and falsifiable. It was Karl Popper (1902-1994) who first pointed out that a statement is scientific only if it is falsifiable. If it is not falsifiable it is not a valid scientific statement. Even so, there are limits to the validity of any scientific statement, and such limits define its domain of validity. The domain of validity of any scientific statement only becomes apparent when the limits have been reached, that is, when the expected result does not occur.

Ideally, scientific method consists of respect for observation, experiment, evidence and testability, as outlined above. However, its 'facts' are not true absolutely but only relatively, under certain specified conditions, limited to a particular domain. Readers may recall Boyle's Law, which fails to hold at very low temperatures.

As a matter of fact, scientific methods are not wholly reliable, dependent as they are on the skill and integrity of the experimenter. Scientific theory, although perfect in itself, is never more than an approximation to the perfection of actuality. This makes it all the more astonishing that its applications have changed our world so fundamentally.

Science should not be idealised. It has its own limitations and is more messy than people believe. Sometimes, theory turns out to be slightly inaccurate and *ad hoc* additions have to be made to the expression of a law. For example, the speed of the galaxies furthest from us is greater than would be expected and in order to align theory with practical experience, what is called 'dark matter' has been invented, although it is not (as yet) visible. This is to account for the acceleration of the galaxies and although it seems like a trick, it is not quite that. Everybody knows that it is an *ad hoc* invention and that it is temporarily in place until improvements can be made or the present somewhat unsatisfactory theory is overturned and replaced.

This is completely different from the additions to religious doctrine such as the Vatican's assertion some years ago that the Virgin Mary had been assumed up to heaven just as Jesus had been. Or that the immaculate conception by the Virgin Mary went back an unlimited number of generations, thus making the nature of Mary totally immaculate. These became articles of faith which *ad hoc* scientific insertions are not.

Another problem about the absolute reliability of scientific data resides in the scientific papers published in learned journals. These have to have approval by a recognised authority in the field in question and so have great authority. What about those papers which are not in line with current thinking, which may be heterodox and explore new ground? There are many papers which go unpublished and which may well have a positive content despite the rejection of the reader. And it seems that it is not unknown for data to be falsified.

Moreover, scientific theory is an abstraction, often expressed mathematically and is, therefore, a form of myth. Would anyone then be justified in treating it as equivalent to other myths such as the story of creation in Genesis? No, because of the manifest differences, despite the shortcomings of science. Even though the truths of science are only relative (conditional), they are valid within the appropriate domain even after they have been shown to be invalid outside. This is not so for religious ideas. Whatever its shortcomings, scientific method has the right to be termed 'miraculous'. It emerged as a way for humanity to relate to the universe and provided the conditions under which applications of science have immeasurably changed humankind's material circumstances.

Most importantly, it has been the means of transforming human consciousness and, reciprocally, has been transformed by the same emergent human consciousness. In making no claim to unchanging, absolute truth but recognising its own relativity/provisionality, the validity of its truths only within particular domains, science possesses a modesty undreamed of in any other form of knowledge system.

Reference to the limitations of science and its methods is, of course, not the whole story. It is still the case that however many times you try the experiment, acid will always turn blue litmus paper red or pink. And there is the famous case of prediction in the eighteenth century when astronomers, turning their telescopes to the heavens, detected perturbations in the movements of the planets which could only be accounted for by assuming the presence of another planet, previously unknown and never before seen because it was so far from us. Using Newtonian theory they predicted its position in the sky at a certain future time when it would be as close as possible, and sure enough, when telescopes were focussed on that particular point in space, there was Pluto, ready and waiting to be discovered in the expected place at the right time.

Experimenters may not be perfect, peer reviewers may sometimes be wrong, a mathematical theory can only approximate to actuality, but science is still not a myth like others: it is an 'informative myth'. It is a myth in constant touch with reality. Space travellers have gone to the moon. Premature babies have been enabled to live. And billions on the planet use mobile phones.

And it is not only the positive achievements which affirm the (relative) validity of scientific truths – the monstrous horrors emerging when power-hungry establishments get their hands on the means of waging warfare or torturing enemies are also demonstrations of validity.

Moreover, scientists and others are constantly on their guard to find fault, to detect mistakes/errors, and on the lookout to improve things, to make changes for the better. In other words, they are prepared and ready to jettison what is wrong and replace it. They are sceptics in the best sense of the word. A hallmark of the scientific enterprise is the pressing need to overturn and replace; to define the domain of validity; or to recognise limitations and overcome them.

Thus, scientific method is intrinsically revolutionary. No sooner is a result established on the basis of testable evidence than there is a look-out for boundaries to the validity of the result, whereupon it will be overturned and replaced.

The resulting sense of freedom offered by the scientific enterprise must be the greatest possible encouragement to inventiveness and creativity.

The principles of scientific method as described in textbooks may be another form of myth but there is an almost miraculous correspondence between the expression of scientific data either in words or in mathematical symbols on the one hand and the events of actuality on the other. The description of the method may be an idealisation but when predictions are fulfilled it may feel like magic. Finding the limits of the validity of any theory is in itself a positive discovery.

Such relativity/provisionality is one of the great glories of science. Therefore, despite its untidiness and the possibility of cul-de-sacs, there is a built-in check on human frailty. And this is so in spite of the social context in which people are inadequate, and in which powerful business interests and corrupt governments often play a reactionary role. On the other hand, the hallmark of religion for its adherents is its absoluteness without possibility of falsification.

It took a long time for a fully formed concept of scientific method to emerge and it was not until the nineteenth century, after physics, chemistry, biology and geology had become recognised sciences that it was fully formalised. We take it so much for granted that we forget what a fruitful human creation it is. And we often forget how it rescues us from the dangers of absolutism and dogmatism. What a threat it seemed to be to theology and God-fearing respectability, though. In his book *Father and Son,* Edmund Gosse quotes his fundamentalist father, who said that fossils were put into the earth by God in order to test people's faith.

Before the Scientific Revolution of the Seventeenth Century

Science as we know it did not emerge until the beginning of the seventeenth century and the first signal of its imminent arrival (although no one would have realised it at the time!) was in the field of astronomy and the implications were cosmological.

Since the time of the ancient world, in Western Europe man had been seen as the centre of the universe, inhabiting an earth (itself at the centre of the universe) which had been created by God and upon which God constantly kept an eye and which was, in fact, God's central object of interest. This was expressed by and supported by models set out by Aristotle (384 – 322 BC) and Ptolemy (AD90 – c.AD168). Both these models had the earth at centre-stage, more-or-less, but Aristotle's was more physical than Ptolemy's, which was geometrical.

Aristotle's picture had the sun and all the planets encased in crystal spheres, which produced their own music as the heavenly bodies went round and round. A beautiful idea which is still enshrined in Milton's line: 'Ring out ye crystal spheres'. Ptolemy's model, although it was geometrical, involved a very complicated arrangement of different circles large and small. When different planets moved round different circles of different sizes at different speeds, the way in which these bodies moved corresponded very largely to astronomical observations, made with pre-telescopic instruments. The model, however, became increasingly out of step with reality in the form of observations.

At that time, the categories of thought were different from today. Instead of seeing the universe in terms of matter moving in space and time, they saw things in terms of substance, form and the essence of things. Events were governed by teleology, that is, determined by (God's) purpose. Their picture was not determined by observation or experiment but was *a priori*, governed by theological considerations. The concept of cause and effect was still governed by Aristotle's notion that the cause of anything was its purpose. The church interpreted this as God's purpose.

The Scientific Revolution of the Seventeenth Century

The crucial date in this story is 1543, the year in which Nicolas Copernicus (1473 – 1543) published *De Revolutionibus Orbium Coelestium* (On The Revolution of the Heavenly Bodies), in which he put forward the hypothesis that it would be mathematically simpler to treat the solar system as if the sun were at its centre rather than the earth having that pride of place as had been the case for over 2,000 years. This (together with a multitude of other factors) set in motion a monumental change in how humanity viewed the world.

There had been previous suggestions in the Greek and also in the Arab worlds but these had not been relevant to the needs and circumstances of the times. In 1543, the circumstances were right and Copernicus's suggestion was followed up by others and the implications carried forward. Copernicus set off a revolution in the relationship of the universe to its own working and structure.

The explosion in science known as the Scientific Revolution emerged into the world in this way although its roots went back considerably further. Many different factors came together to facilitate this 'revolution'; social, economic, political and others too numerous to enumerate. All philosophical and religious ideas came to be scrutinised, and unprecedented transformations took place in the spiritual and intellectual spheres. The world, as Christopher Hill wrote, was being 'turned upside down'. In this uncertain and unstable world it seemed as if mathematics was the only source of certainty through the remorseless logic of Euclid's geometry.

Copernicus's great contribution to human thought was to free humanity from the shackles of having to see the universe from a single viewpoint. It freed humanity to change the frame of reference from which one viewed things, at will.

The next important leap was taken by Johannes Kepler (1571 – 1630), who described how the sun and planets were related to each other by means of mathematical (quantitative) laws. One of Kepler's laws stated that the planets move in ellipses (ovals) with the sun at one focus, and this he demonstrated geometrically basing himself on observational results. This broke a longstanding rule that motion in the heavenly sphere must be circular. This rule followed from the conviction that everything in the heavenly sphere must be perfect.

Kepler's better-known contemporary, Galileo, also supported Copernicus and suffered because he was a Roman Catholic in Italy under the Inquisition. Galileo did the unthinkable, he raised his telescope to the sky and exposed the 'scandal' of sun spots, that is, imperfections on the sun. Such sun spots should not have existed because it had long been taken for granted that the celestial sphere was perfect and had no imperfections. This was a truly important breakthrough and opened the way for the whole of the material universe to be treated uniformly in terms of matter moving in space and time.

He also showed, using his newly-invented telescope, that Jupiter, the largest planet in the solar system, had a set of 'moons' circling round it just like the solar system as a whole. Here was an even worse scandal, perhaps. Another solar system in the heavens, seemingly similar to our own. Would this mean other worlds like ours? In that case, what about the unique place of man in the cosmos, for there might have to be, for example, another Jesus Christ to redeem other forms of life.

Closer to home, Galileo put his talents to work in things like bending beams, pendulums and bodies sliding down inclined planes. Galileo's treatment of these phenomena was purely quantitative and these bodies were treated as matter subject to forces, moving in space and time. The same happened in his treatment of falling bodies. No longer were they to be seen as falling to the ground faster and faster because their natural place was at the centre of the earth and they were anxious to get to their natural place. Such qualitative, teleological notions are replaced by simple cause and effect such as we are familiar with.

The climax to this process of quantification and 'mechanisation' occurs with the work of Isaac Newton in his monumental work *Philosophiae Naturalis Principia Mathematica (The Mathematical Principles of Natural Philosophy)*. In the *Principia*, a remorselessly logical theory applicable to the whole universe was laid out and expressed geometrically in mathematical laws for all the bodies in the solar system. The force of attraction holding things together is gravity. Newton claimed to be strictly experimental and denied ever using anything hypothetical. [Readers will remember that John Locke (1632-1704), the great English empiricist philosopher, was a contemporary, so George Fox expressed the spirit of the times with his 'experiential' or 'experimental' basis for belief.] God has not disappeared from the scene, however. In the minds of the scientists of that time he is still behind the scenes as the great original creator and scientific work was carried out to 'the greater glory of God'.

Newton's methods are exciting in themselves. For example, at one time he had a problem in deciding what to take as the distance between two spherical bodies. Was it the distance between their centres? Or was it the distance between the points on their circumferences farthest away from each other? Or was it the distance between the points on their circumferences nearest to each other? The matter was decided by Newton proving that any homogeneous spherical body could be treated as if it were a point at its own centre with a mass equal to the mass of the body as a whole. Could anything be more perfect in its logicality?

The important thing is, however, that for Newton, science consisted of laws stating the mathematical behaviour of nature and such laws were deducible from phenomena, that is, happenings which may be observed and recorded in experiment. Through his work, the entire cosmos becomes knowable, continuous, deterministic, predictable and subject to cause and effect. And yet all of them, from Copernicus to Newton himself, were deeply religious.

Over and above this, the algebraic notation in which science was to be expressed had been invented and was ready and waiting to be used as a vehicle for expressing scientific laws. Perhaps this is not surprising. After all, science now involved the abstraction of the quantitative aspect from any situation and once this was the case, algebraic notation would be the perfect vehicle in which to express its results. Everything slotted in beautifully.

Furthermore, algebraic expressions are both general and potentially particular. Not only was algebra able to express general laws but it was possible to take particular values of (assign numbers to) the variables corresponding to particular experimental results. And the algebra expressing the scientific results was connected with, independent of and indifferent to the physical reality it was relating to. How did this all work out so well?

Perhaps it was mainly because of the embeddedness of potentially mathematical relationships in the physical world? At the same time, I must recognise that countless factors were at work driving events forward and, however engaging I find this story of a scientific revolution, it is a logical reconstruction of a great deal of trial and error.

The Legacy of Newton

Newton and others following him made certain assumptions about the world which affected later science and thinking considerably, until the end of the nineteenth century. The Newtonian world was mechanistic. It was the world of a celestial clockmaker who started it off and left it, only interfering periodically to put things right. As a condition for experimental work, subject and object independence was assumed as a condition for the objectivity of experimental data. And it was very much a deterministic world whose future could in principle be predicted by knowing the condition of all bodies and the forces acting on them at the present time.

This was a world in which bodies were separated from each other by boundaries which the experimenter could decide at will. Cause and effect were clearly delineated and it was assumed that every effect must have a cause. Fragmentation was the order of the day on the basis of the whole being equal to the sum of the parts.

Later, in chemistry, different levels emerged which it was assumed were independent of each other. The model was reductionist and the basis was atomic, all 'higher' levels being dependent on it and determined by it. It would not be until the twentieth century that 'top down determinism' was recognised as playing a reciprocal role to this. In pre-twentieth century science, experimental results were indisputable and determinism and certainty were the rule. It was taken for granted that there is perfect correspondence between theory and physical reality.

Into the Modern World

Unfortunately, this exposition has involved a lot of factual detail. This was inevitable in order to make clear the extraordinary events which coincided to transform the world and, therefore, to make clear the apparently miraculous leap in human consciousness. There may be theists who would jump on my use of the word 'miracle' and assert that I must now admit the intervention of God in all these occurrences. However, this cannot be the case.

For why should God wait until the middle of the sixteenth century to make clear to people that the sun, not the earth, is the centre of the universe when the universe has been in existence for more than thirteen billion years? And I do not use the word 'miracle' in the biblical sense but as a word sufficiently extreme in its meaning to convey the extremity of the transformation. It refers to what Marxists would call a qualitative change.

In the centuries which followed, other sciences such as chemistry, physics and biology broke through similarly and by the end of the nineteenth century, science had become almost complacent and it seemed as if soon there would be 'a theory of everything'. But this was not to be. It was at this time that the theory(ies) of relativity (special and general) and quantum theory were born and, a little later, Hubble discovered the ideology-shattering fact of the expanding universe. At the turn of the twentieth century, science revealed its own relativity and the full implications of scientific method when all sorts of assumptions were called into question and had to be overturned and replaced.

The expanding universe had disconcerting implications and questions arising. Most of such questions are in the domain of science and may or may not be answered satisfactorily in the course of time. Others are answered by theists in terms of their various religions. We do not know how the universe began: a 'bubble' in a pre-existing universe? An emergence from another universe of higher dimensions? Out of nothing? There is ample space here for the religious to fill with God. If the universe is expanding, what is it expanding into? What is the nature of the origin of the expansion? Why is it expanding? Will it go on for ever? Or will it eventually start contracting? If so, why? If not, why not? Is our expanding universe merely one out of countless universes each expanding and contracting in an infinite series of pulsations? The so-called Big Bang is by no means a foregone conclusion and scientists are constantly considering other possibilities.

Then, there are the questions relating to our place in this expanding universe. Before Copernicus, the earth was taken to be the centre with 'man' living on it and seen to be surveyed with enormous and exclusive interest by God who was (on the outside) in the heavens. After this, the sun took pride of place and then the galaxy. Is there a centre and, if so, where is it?

We have known for a long time now how small we on this planet are in comparison with the size of cosmic space and how insignificant. Hubble's expanding universe added another dimension to this. We are clinging on to our planet, which is a relatively small part of the solar system, which is at the edge of our galaxy. 'Where' is our galaxy? Has the universe a 'centre'? Is this concept appropriate in this context? It is tempting to imagine the cosmos as a gigantic sphere expanding with ourselves somewhere in it. But where? It turns out that we really do not know where we are – and this in a very real sense. We might be anywhere. We might be at any point in the cosmos. We might be at the circumference. We might even, at the end of the road, be at the centre after all.

Theory of Relativity

About 400 years separate Copernicus from Einstein (1879 - 1955). In that time, human categories of thought had been totally transformed as had humanity's material existence, at least in certain parts of the world. However, a particular concept links these two thinkers, that of relativity, albeit in slightly different forms. Copernicus freed people from the constraint of a single frame of reference originating at the centre of a spherical earth by moving the centre to the sun. This implied a world of different frames of reference, each resulting in a different model but equally valid. Ptolemy's earth-centred model of the universe in the ancient world had equal validity to the sun-centred one of Copernicus although the latter was mathematically simpler. In any case, in everyday life we have to live as if the earth were at rest and the sun were going round it.

Einstein's special theory of relativity has something in common with this. If there are two frames of reference (two bodies moving relative to each other with constant speed), an observer in each frame of reference will measure mass, length and time differently (that is, they will get different answers when they do the measurements). For example, if there are two flashes of light they will appear to be simultaneous or not depending on whether they are observed in the first or the second frame of reference. What must always be taken into account is the relationship of events and processes to the observer.

The special theory of relativity demonstrated that all measurements must be considered in relation to (relative to) the circumstances of the observer concerned. Even in the simple case of the two flashes of light which appear simultaneous to one observer, they will appear to happen at different times relative to another observer moving relative to the first. And this applies to measurements of length, time, mass and so on.

Perhaps the most significant thing here is that each observer thinks of herself/himself as the one who is not moving and thinks of the other one as the one in motion. So each one thinks that they are the absolute frame of reference. This relativity does not mean that the absolute is abolished, however. It does not mean that 'everything is relative'. The occurrence of the event is still an absolute. *What is relative is the measurement.*

In case anyone thinks that this makes a difference to our daily lives, it does not. The differences are only apparent at velocities approaching that of light. When we are moving at 'normal' speeds on the surface of the earth, everything is as we are used to. Einstein's equations approach closer and closer to those of Newton as the relative velocities of the observers get smaller and smaller. Furthermore, in everyday life we do not even assume that the earth goes round the sun. We live every day as if the earth were at the centre of the solar system and as if the earth were flat.

The idea of the relative and the absolute were prominent in the late nineteenth century in philosophy as well as in physics, much more so than ever before. But the formulation of this particular theory by Albert Einstein was based on an assumption calling for particular intellectual courage. This was the courage required to make an assumption that appeared to contradict common sense. This assumption was that light has the same velocity relative to any observer, no matter how fast that observer is travelling. This is equivalent to saying that if a train is travelling along a track, it does not matter how fast it is going, another train will always pass it at the same relative speed.

The exciting thing is the grasping of this contradiction as the only possibility that made sense. When special relativity was tested over large distances and high velocities, the theory was experimentally verified – and yet, and yet ... It is difficult to think about and hard to believe in many ways. And it is certainly expressed in very abstract mathematics. For some physicists doubts remain to this day.

Why is this point being made here in relation to nontheism? It is not only that the abstractness of the theory scales the very heights of human intellectual possibilities. It is not simply the joy obtained from the mastery of such a theory when this is possible. It is also that the scientific world takes for granted the provisional character of scientific theory. However hallowed the ideas, however respected their originator, at the end of the road if experiment queries the result, we shall have to look at everything again and, if necessary, reshape it.

After almost 200 years in which Newton had been almost deified, it was accepted that Newton's laws are valid only in the domain of small distances and speeds and do not apply outside these limits. They have to give way to those of Einstein, which are valid in a domain of high speeds and large distances. What an outstanding demonstration of the power of scientific method.

And, of course, the relevance to nontheism lies yet again in the contrast with the absoluteness and dogmatism of religion. Paradoxically, the admission of the possibility of human fallibility in the scientific field demonstrates a deep respect for human dignity and creativity. Perhaps this is the real connection with nontheism and it would apply to any scientific field.

One last point. General relativity (which is concerned with gravity, acceleration and space curvature) calls for such highly abstract mathematics that it does call into question the theist idea of an intelligent designer. In order to express the ideas of general relativity an abstract entity known as a tensor has to be invented. And there is a branch of algebra called tensor calculus. Tensors are the abstract tools by which the mathematics of general relativity is teased out and they are, as has been said, highly abstract - many degrees more abstract than the sort of algebraic quantities familiar to the general reader.

What comes to mind is the question: granted it would call for a very *mathematically intelligent* designer to create a universe requiring tensor calculus, why would such a designer choose such a convoluted and obscure method of creation so that it needed the genius of one particular person in the early twentieth century to work it all out? And did the designer choose the particular individual concerned? Such questions may seem flippant (and perhaps they are flippant) but there are implications here that call for an answer.

Quantum Theory

The second major innovation in physical science at the beginning of the twentieth century was quantum theory. Where relativity dealt in the very large (velocities and spaces), quantum theory dealt in minute particles, smaller than the atom. But this was not the only way in which they differed. Quantum theory was enormously more revolutionary than relativity, which preserved determinism and the old, classical notions of cause and effect.

This is why readers are asked to exert more patience here because a few more pages of 'facts' are needed to enable them to grasp just how revolutionary quantum theory was (and is).

In experiments at this subatomic level, we do not actually see what happens to the electrons, the tiny subatomic particles on which we experiment. We do our 'observations' with an ultramicroscope and all we see is the 'trace' of the motion of the electron on a screen; the graph on the screen which models its motion. We can only perceive at the everyday level of existence so that anything subatomic can only be seen via the microscope which projects an image only on a screen. The image on the screen is at our experiential level of perception.

More importantly, perhaps, we have the mathematics of the motion of the electron and this we 'see' directly and immediately. There is no barrier between us and the equations! How extraordinary that, unable to 'reach' the electron which we are 'observing', we can construct the equations which map its motion. The universe, unable to see the electron which is part of itself and which it is observing, can construct, out of its very own being, the equation which is also part of itself.

Furthermore, what the electron appears to do is determined largely by the apparatus we set up and on what the apparatus is designed to investigate. The electron behaves like a particle when it reacts with a position-measuring device and like a wave when it is observed via an apparatus designed to detect waves. It is as if the electron does not know what it is or how it will behave until it reaches the measuring device – or, to put it rather dramatically, the experiment is a 'dynamic unfolding of possibilities'. The possibilities become actualities when we observe/measure that which we have set out to observe/measure.

Note the decisive role of the subject/observer in deciding what will actualise. We have lost absolute determinism but relative determinism remains. What happens depends upon the conditions encountered by the electron. At this level, the world is one of relatively unlimited possibilities transformed into actualities when we make our observations.

This is clear in the subatomic realm, the scale of which is such that even one photon ('atom' of light) makes a real difference, but although this must also be the case at the macro-level, it is not noticeable. The transformation from potentiality into actuality at the level of ordinary experience must be so indescribably fast, and the scale of things is such that the world we perceive appears as continuous and solid.

Scientific discoveries did not come to an end after the emergence of quantum theory early in the twentieth century. What is relevant to our discussion is the discovery of an enormous number of new particles. These, it seems, can 'pop up' unexpectedly and often die after an unbelievably short life!

At the moment, it seems that scientists are trying to observe the so-called Higgs boson which, it is said, will enable them to understand the nature of matter itself. It appears that a Higgs boson is a particle manifestation of a Higgs field, that is, a field of high energy. A Higgs boson interacts with tiny entities ('particles') to give mass to these things.

It was in 1927 that Werner Heisenberg (1901 – 1976), a well-known atomic physicist, published his findings which included the Heisenberg Uncertainty Principle or Heisenberg Indeterminacy Principle. It is this: for a moving particle like an electron, which has both position and velocity, it is impossible to measure both of these with 100% accuracy simultaneously. To measure the position, you would have to reduce it to rest and cannot measure the velocity, but to measure the velocity it would have to keep moving and you could not accurately fix the position. We have now lost absolute objectivity, absolute determinacy, total predictability and causality, all in a few short years.

From the Everyday World to the Quantum World

Quantum theory is more revolutionary than relativity because relativity leaves causality, determinism and predictability untouched. The Heisenberg indeterminacy (uncertainty) principle means that the electron has a position and a velocity which cannot be accurately measured simultaneously. All that we have are probabilities.

What a contrast to Newtonian physics, whose entities have clearly defined and predictable paths and are seen as having definite positions and to be travelling with definite velocities. Here, causality and determinism are basic assumptions. The classical (Newtonian) world has continuously varying quantities and the experimenter can determine the relationship between variables earlier and later. The disturbance due to the apparatus can be made arbitrarily small so as to be ignored.

The quantum world is different. All we 'really' know are the mathematical equations involved. We cannot see the electron we are supposed to be experimenting with, only its trace on a screen at our own level of everyday experience. Absolute predictability has gone, to be replaced by probabilities. This is a world of discontinuity in which particles can 'pop up' unheralded and with no apparent cause. Continuity and discreteness are relative and what appears as continuous at the level of the everyday is not so at a different level.

This is a truly revolutionary transformation - no wonder that Einstein refused to accept it. What is really surprising is that quantum theory has proved so successful in its applications, despite all the apparent problems. In fact, there is a sort of naked reality about the quantum level. It seems to bring us to a sort of 'edge' of the universe and this apparent 'boundary' character is what leads us on seductively to expect it to be close to answering very basic questions.

This expectation is increased when we take quantum theory together with relativity. At one end, we are in touch with the very large and at the other with the very small. Have we reached boundaries? Are there such things as boundaries? How can there be? Perhaps the cosmos *is* self-referring? Only time and further work will tell.

All this speaks to the human spirit. What is conjured up by modern physical theory is a world of 'terrible beauty'. However, such beauty is expressed in mathematics which is highly abstract – its beauty is of a different character from the physics which it models. The equations in which the physical universe is ultimately modelled are of breathtaking simplicity. It might well be said that the real beauty of physics and cosmology lies in the mathematics in which it is expressed.

Twentieth and twenty-first century science has leapt ahead of anything that has gone before and in ways which could not have been anticipated. This has been notably the case in the field of biology. Physics and cosmology have been extended in many ways but have not resulted in more revolutionary theory. The old classical world has certainly not disappeared for it provides valid assumptions for how the world works at the level of the everyday. There are still cause and effect, determinism, rationality, objectivity and clearly defined objects at the level of the everyday. Newtonian cosmology is still valid within the domain of the solar system. However, that is within the limited sphere of everyday experience. At the deeper level it is indeterminate, unpredictable, self-referential, relativistic, ambiguous and paradoxical. And the two levels coexist in what appears to be a contradictory manner. This is a classical case of the necessity to grasp the contradiction in order to grasp the total reality.

We know, however, that the contradiction is only apparent and that the different appearances and forms of behaviour at the two different levels simply depend on the frame of reference from which we take our stand. The fascinating thing is that our understanding of behaviour at both levels depends upon human perception and is constructed out of it. Fortunately, we are rescued from subjectivity (even solipsism) by the undeniable fact that all perception and thinking is, itself, part of the 'objective' universe.

The theoretical glory of science still lies in the possibility of its expression in mathematical terms, which makes possible the other aspect of its glory, its predictive power and, therefore, its applicability, apparently miraculously, in all human life. 'Nothing comes from nothing' was once accepted as indisputable but today this seems to be contradicted by the emergence and growth of our modern world over a relatively short period of time out of (virtually) nothing.

What skill, imagination, hard work and courage it has taken in order for this to happen. The most admirable aspect has been the courage needed by innovators to risk social opprobrium, physical suffering or even death at certain times and under certain circumstances. What would it have been like to be born into the world of heavenly spheres and Aristotelian physics and to have to summon up the courage to risk the consequences of thinking and transcending an outmoded world-outlook? Despite all the faults and shortcomings of today's world no one risks being burned alive for accepting quantum theory.

And yet this world is quite different from the one we are used to. It seems that at this subatomic level everything behaves differently from the ways we would expect and have hitherto taken for granted. It is a world of 'pop-up' particles without apparent cause; of electrons whose behaviour is the result of how we observe them and unlike our old, predictable, measurable Newtonian universe, a world in which the position and velocity of a particle cannot be simultaneously determined by the initial conditions to 100% accuracy.

The work has been done, the experiments have been performed, the results have been recorded and we are asked to accept the seemingly impossible. What sort of rationalism is that? And although these categories are not a part of the experiment at the level of measurements, it seems that, philosophically, the behaviour of the electron takes us back to the medieval world of the transformation of potentiality into actuality.

Perhaps the real hero(ine) of this story is scientific method. For, if we take the scientific picture of our universe as a whole, from the very small to the very large, it encompasses both the causal and the contingent, the potential and the actual. It has given back in a more precise form what we knew to be the case at the beginning.

It is at this point that it seems we are at the boundary of our universe in some sort of way and are on the brink of something totally different. Theists may well (and they do) ask us to agree, on the basis of a quantum world so different from the ordinary, everyday one, that we have to admit that there may well be something 'out there' totally different from the three-dimensional, measurable world of matter, space and time. What is our answer? This is quite simple and repeats what we have said so many times before: humanity will continue to press on investigating the cosmos and we look forward to what emerges, whatever it is, but we will not anticipate what this may be by a sort of guesswork based upon our own conditioning, prejudices and need for comfort, love and meaning.

Modern Scientific 'Mystics'

What motivated hard-working scientists to achieve what they did? The answer to this comes from an unexpected source, the creators of relativity and quantum theory themselves. They were in every real sense of the word 'mystics' although they rarely, if ever, mentioned a possible deity or creator. Their non-scientific writings demonstrate their attitudes to the universe.

Einstein actually wrote about his concept of God, which was a developmental one. He saw the earliest concept of God as one based on fear from which a second stage emerged later. This stage was social, moral and anthropomorphic. The third (and for Einstein, final stage) was a 'cosmic religious feeling' which was not anthropomorphic. Such a feeling, he thought, could not give rise to a definite idea of God nor any theology so he concluded that the most important function of art and science was to awaken such a feeling. How lovely that he bracketed science together with art. We are accustomed to refer to applied science and technology simply as 'science' and it is not right to do so. Science is theoretical, conceptual; a collection of models of physical reality and, as such, a form of or branch of art.

How spiritually refreshing it is to have someone like Einstein saying that the main function of science is not to provide material comforts but to awake spiritual consciousness. He may be exaggerating somewhat but he has the right idea. He calls himself a 'religious nonbeliever'.

He writes:

> 'I maintain that the cosmic religious feeling is the strongest and noblest motive for scientific research.'

Further:

> 'How can cosmic religious feeling be communicated from one person to another if it can give rise to no definite notion of a God and no theology? In my view, it is the most important function of art and science to awaken this feeling and keep it alive in those who are receptive to it.' *(New York Times Magazine, November 9, 1930, pp.1-4.)*

Einstein was by no means alone in these views. Louis de Broglie (1892 - 1987), a major contributor to quantum theory, also seems to have been motivated by spiritual ideals with no transcendental implications. The pursuit of science is a huge effort, he writes, and if asked the question: what makes it worthwhile, his reply is that it is the goal of knowledge of natural phenomena and of establishing rational relations among them '*independent of all utilitarian preoccupations*'. [My emphases].

He writes of the 'unique pleasure of having a momentary glimpse of some new aspect of truths …' (*Quantum Questions. Mystical Writings of the World's Great Physicists*, ed. Ken Wilber, Shambhala, Boston, 1984). Such a description resonates totally with the experience we all have had, at an infinitely more modest level, of a sudden new insight into something we had never understood before.

He (unwittingly?) makes another nonreligious reference using a word usually reserved for a religious context: '… that bold act of faith' leading us to believe in a correlation between thoughts or pictures in the mind and the things or phenomena around us. If we stop for a moment to think about this, we realise that this is, indeed, an act of faith, unexpected though the notion is in this context. If asked why this should be so, it would not be unreasonable to suggest that the thoughts are an aspect of the scientist who is herself/himself part of what the thoughts are embedded in. And this applies also to the expression of the physical relationships in mathematical, symbolic form. The physicist (part of the universe) expresses the physical relations embedded in the universe in mathematical symbols created by the mathematician (who is also part of the universe).

Max Planck (1858 – 1947), another hero of quantum theory, emphasises the role of imagination in the scientific enterprise and explains that the scientist must start with an 'imaginative picture' of the law he is pursuing and this must be embodied in an imaginary hypothesis. This is absolutely indispensable. Reason alone is not enough.

So it turns out that what is needed to achieve the greatest heights of scientific discovery are insights of a spiritual character, acts of faith and imaginary hypotheses. Who would have thought it? And we have it from their own mouths – with no reference to the need for any deities. The sheer spiritual joyfulness of these people with respect to the universe and their relationship to it through their scientific work speaks for itself. Very few of us are blessed with the ability to accomplish what they did but this makes no difference. We can experience equal inspiration from anything we accomplish or try to accomplish. Or from so much else. And without selling our intellectual or spiritual independence.

How astonishing and wonderful it is that science, a quantitative abstraction which gives no information about the things most dear to us, that is, music, colour, joy, tragedy, beauty, pity and so forth, because it is an abstraction which has eliminated the qualitative, should deliver such spiritual joy.

Something out of nothing?

Of course, science has transformed the lives of millions

in countless ways too many to enumerate and too well-known to need enumeration. However, these giants of scientific theory remind us of the unlimited creativity of human consciousness and its ability in so many different fields to create something out of nothing.

To use the phrase 'something out of nothing' might seem like an overstatement. Surely the phrase must mean that something is created out of an absolute 'void/emptiness'? Yet this very void/emptiness always exists under certain conditions or within certain boundaries? Do these play a role in the creative process? Can the void itself play such a role? It sometimes does seem that something comes out of nothing. After all, before scientific theory existed there was no scientific theory. Before there were numeral signs such symbols did not exist and had to be created.

Previous to such creation, what existed was human consciousness/mind on one hand, and on the other, the total milieu both social and natural. What was created emerged from the *relationship* between mind and milieu, not from the milieu alone or mind alone. Relationship is not a thing, it is a noetic/mental entity. It is a no-thing. There is no science or mathematics until there is the right *relationship* between mind and milieu. It is in this sense that we have the right to assert that people created science and mathematics (and much else) out of nothing.

It might be asserted with considerable justification that this is not genuinely 'something out of nothing' because the prerequisite, the necessary conditions, for such creation is the pre-existence of consciousness and the milieu. But these, on their own, do not provide the sufficient conditions for the creation. They provide only the necessary conditions. The sufficient conditions are provided when consciousness/mind is seeking for something significant in the context concerned. Mind and milieu are then brought together in the right relationship, *no-thing* has been added. Something new has emerged out of the (non-material) *relationship* between mind/consciousness and the milieu.

This applies to all human creation at all times and in all parts of the world. Perhaps the most outstanding human creativity was exerted at the dawn of history when 'something' was created out of 'nothing' by our earliest ancestors. All of us should salute these people who made life as we now know it a possibility.

Chapter 6

Gathering the Threads Together

One conclusion may be drawn from Meister Eckhart's saying: 'Why dost thou prate of God? Everything thou sayest of him is false.' That conclusion is that we are all, theists and nontheists alike, in the same boat. There are a lot of things we (all of us) do not know. The advantage we possess as nontheists is that we know that we do not know and we admit this openly. Moreover, although we all build models to represent what we think we know, theists and nontheists alike, we part company over the different nature of our models. Models such as the theory of evolution may be falsified but religious models are not subject to falsification. Whatever happens, however tragic, however appalling, it is the will of God who 'moves in a mysterious way'.

Another aspect of this is the diversity of approaches to belief as such. People are searching for meaning in their lives and are finding it in a variety of non-institutional ways. Although it is not always verbalised, deep down there is a real yearning for answers to the big questions and for many people the answers provided by the established religions are totally unsatisfactory. It is simplistic to say that most people need to feel loved; they need others to love, they want to feel safe, they want to be appreciated, encouraged and (in the final analysis) do not want to die. The need for meaning (which includes explanation) may be an overpowering one.

Belief in some sort of mythology as if it were 'true', that is 'factual' cannot be simply dismissed by logical arguments and scientific knowledge. Loss of belief spells loss of meaning in life, the opening up of an abyss, an emptiness, the horror of nothingness. Without their religious beliefs many people would feel their lives to be pointless; they would feel deep pain confronted by the apparent indifference of the universe; they would feel abandoned, uncertain, empty.

For some of us, though, there is an extraordinary beauty in 'nothingness' and deep satisfaction to be obtained from the idea of unfathomable depths. What does it feel like to be an atheist or nontheist? It feels great. It feels free. It means standing on one's own feet. Richard Holloway uses 'atheising' as the word for the process of ridding the mind of conceptual idols. And it is well to bear in mind that any concept, not only religious ones, may become idolised and may become an obstacle to contact with reality. It is hard, if not impossible, to contemplate the non-material and, almost inevitably, we construct an image for what is unimaginable.

Most of us obtain great spiritual joy from music, art, poetry or the love of friends, family or nature. Such secular spirituality takes us to the very edge of 'absolute knowing' but it must be admitted that it is unlikely to console us for the loss of a loved one or remove the fear of our own death. This is the possible downside of nontheism. Each of us has to balance the gains and losses but, for myself, I would not trade my intellectual and spiritual freedom for the illusion of security.

We need explanations about a multitude of things, even a reason why we are here at all and religion provides various forms of explanation, all of which differ from one another. One thing they have in common, though, is their way of stating these as if there were total authority behind them (with the possible exception of Buddhism). And the sense of authority appeals to many who do not see the colonisation and dictatorship of the soul implied by the claim of unique revelation. Afraid of chance, uncertainty and unpredictability, religious believers are in danger of selling their souls for the illusion of security offered by the social milieu which enfolded them as babies and then helped them to survive by looking after them. And their noblest idealism is exploited in order to capture and control their intellects, hearts and souls. It is nothing short of a sort of spiritual imperialism.

We do, indeed, need stories or myths, but why do they have to be presented as if they were historical facts when it is manifestly obvious that they are not? It is not that aspect which is the most important, however. The worst aspect is that such myths render the recipient helpless in the face of authority. This need not be the case. I find the narrative of the history of ideas enthralling, not to say empowering, especially the history of scientific ideas. One might say that a historian of science is the universe finding out how it discovered its own workings. But even the history of scientific ideas has its mythical aspect, and it derives from the abstraction of a tidy, purposeful, directed narrative from a messy, untidy reality.

A New Spirituality

What of the future? What may it hold if it turns out that humanity does survive against all odds? We have all learned not to make predictions, as we know now that whatever we think may happen almost certainly will not. There is an unlimited number of things which are possible and what does occur will certainly not be what we expect because we cannot know all the contingent factors which will help to determine the future. Nevertheless, there is no harm in trying to sketch out the broad outlines of what we would like to see as humanity's spiritual future.

There is no question that humanity needs a new spirituality to replace the out-of-date stories treated as historical facts and the primitive morality of the old, tired belief systems that have outlived their credibility and been shamefully used in order to promote misogyny, racism, exploitation and universal oppression.

The new spirituality needs to be grown-up, serious and honest. Strange though it may sound, what is needed is a secular spirituality (for the 'religious nonbeliever' as Einstein described himself). And there is ample scope for the emergence and development of a variety of forms of secular spirituality in today's world.

Spirituality resides in the relational aspect of human experience. 'Meaning', that elusive but essential component to our lives that we all yearn for, resides in the types of relationships we have. The latter may be identified with the human spirit. This is just like the word 'prayer' which might have two meanings, its usual one and also, if you look hard enough at it, it means pray-er, the one who prays. Thus, meaning corresponds to this in being like the totality of human relationships, i.e. the human spirit.

At the same time, we can only relate to the universe when we (the Subjects) are separate from the universe (the Object). When the Subject is identified with the Object we cannot relate, only experience immediately, intuit if you like, but we cannot reflect upon it or relate to it. However, at the moment when the Subject comes to know or becomes aware of some aspect of the Object (universe), there is an instant of identity between Subject and Object and at that instant there can be no reflection by the Subject (universe) on the Object (universe), only intuition. At that instant, in a very real sense, the universe knows itself and seems to know everything known to that universe.

What we have called 'spirituality' is not an entity or 'thing' in any sense, nor is 'spirit'. The problem is that even these words conjure up mental images of some sort, which is almost unavoidable in the three-dimensional world we live in composed of matter, in space and time. We have some sort of image of *no-thing* in spite of ourselves. We should not try and replace such images by visual symbols, such as crosses and statues and the repeated words uttered, the formulaic liturgies repeated time and again in services in religious places of worship. These, in their time, become idolatrous.

We need a totally new concept of the human spirit – one that replaces what has passed for the spiritual up till now, one that encompasses the totality of our material as well as non-material existence, the totality of our non-material lives.

Self-Transformation

Let us look at this from the viewpoint of the self-referring universe. We have seen that the universe is in process of becoming more and more aware of itself through the vehicle of conscious beings such as ourselves (and any others who may coexist with us) who are part of that very universe. By this means, the relationship between the universe (as Subject) and the universe (as Object), undergoes constant change.

It is daunting to see that it follows that our purpose in being here is creative self-realisation as a channel/vehicle for the self-realisation of the universe. It is even more daunting to know that in thinking/writing this, I am reflecting upon the role that I (and all other people) play in the self-realization of the universe. And I ask myself: is this reflection a level above ordinary self-realisation?

Many of us are fortunate enough at the end of our lives to discover that the results of our reflection, probing, examination and thoughts about, the world, our self-transformation, has brought us to a place which feels blissfully 'at home' in our inner selves. We feel that we have repossessed our inner selves, the original, fresh, untarnished beings that we once were when we started out.

Is this who I really am? It is tempting to think so. However, since my spiritual journey continues beyond this, it cannot be so. Is there a 'real me' which re-emerges late in life after some enlightenment has been achieved by some form of 'winding-down' process and which recaptures the original self which has been distorted in the course of life by social pressures?

It surely cannot be like that since the original self, the core being, has been added to, expanded by experiences, feelings, thoughts.

Perhaps the 'real me' is what I think I should be? Perhaps it is the form I feel most happy with? We are, however, still faced with the initial problem – we can never know at any point in life what is in store for us in the future. Perhaps as we go on we become more and more our real selves as we change into something else?

In the life of every individual, the apparent separation of mind from body has to occur as a necessary condition for going forward spiritually and intellectually. We have to behave *as if* they were separate although it is obviously impossible for this to be the case. This is tantamount to estrangement, or alienation (as Hegel and Marx would have expressed it), of the self as Subject from the self as Object. Awareness, knowing, self-expression are the means for further development and a return to the self, the transcending of alienation, the 'return home'.

Knowing, awareness, and so on by the Subject in relation to the Object involves discovery of aspects of the non-Subject ('Object') which the Subject previously thought of as 'other'. The initial condition for such discovery is the 'externalisation' by the Subject of the aspect of the universe-as-object which it had earlier regarded as 'other'. Activity, reflection, intuiting, and other activities of the Subject reveal the 'otherness' as an illusion. In the act of knowing it is deeply fulfilling to experience the sense of the apparent 'other' being absorbed into the self as a familiar aspect of oneself. Through such self-transformation the Subject and hence the universe realises itself.

Such ideas sound teleological because it seems that the end of the process determines the beginning and the road to be taken. And although purpose is not to be identified with cause (except by Aristotle), a sense of purpose will certainly determine one's choices at any point along the road. The ends of such progress are not absolutely predetermined but only relatively predetermined or else the process would be mechanistic and it is the contingencies relative to the process which rescue the system from this fate. Where are the contingencies in the progression of the universe? These must come from aspects of itself as, by definition, we are talking of the universe, that is everything, and so there cannot be an 'outside'.

What is clear is that, in a self-referring universe, if there is to be self-transformation, that is, self-realisation, there must be (even unconsciously) a form of reflection upon the self. For this to occur there has to be the pretence at separation from the self, we have to behave *as if* we were simultaneously part of and yet separate from the self. We are simultaneously actor and audience. And this recalls the dictum: 'Be ye in this world but not of it'.

A changing consciousness must, any time, involve both Being and Becoming as its principal aspects. And it is hard to keep track of both of these at the same time. In considering the process of development of a Subject's beliefs, we cannot grasp simultaneously the instantaneous belief (Being) and the direction in which it is going (Becoming). When we try to pin down the Being, the Becoming escapes us, and when we try to pin down the Becoming, the Being escapes us - a veritable Heisenberg indeterminacy principle. (See chapter on *Science and the Human Spirit*, p.126).

In the instantaneous act of changing/ developing/ transforming, although the Subject and Object differ beforehand, they are both changed by development. The Subject, through its new awareness, incorporates the Object into itself and, hence, there is a new Subject and a new Object.

This is pretty obvious but what is harder to come to grips with is the question of what are the qualities we wish to aspire to as we transform ourselves in the course of life. And how best do we effect such change? We would aspire to be independent-minded, autonomous, guilt-free, able to balance one's own needs with those of others, compassionate, free-thinking, loving, encouraging to others, positive, with no need of false props or idols, rational, able to set boundaries, see our own spirituality and able totally to transcend race, nationality and other differences in the courageous pursuit of justice for all. In all this, the distinction between the social and so-called spiritual spheres should vanish, to be replaced by a seamless whole. While in today's world we call for the separation of religion and state, we look forward to a single seamless sphere of combined material and individual secular spirituality.

It has already been said by many others: humankind needs a new spirituality; grown-up, honest and fully human and must not be put off by fake substitutes. Moreover, this should be a seamless whole without distinction between different forms of spirituality. All adventures of the human spirit should be recognised as equal to one another irrespective of their particular natures. My need to write this down is, perhaps, my most urgent reason for writing this book.

Development of the Idea of God

The conscious human spirit may be seen as a vehicle for the emergent awareness of the universe as a whole. The universe is absolute and corresponds for some with the idea of God, and throughout history the latter has been transformed with the transformation of consciousness itself. (It is reassuring to think that, if the awareness of the absolute is developmental, there really is progress, despite the postmodernist denial). And it is exhilarating to realise that the absolute itself is impermanent and has its relative aspect.

The most recent concept of God has been devised by the universe through human beings to represent its best, most perfect, infinite and beautiful aspects. Alternatively, it may be seen as the abstraction from all the abstractions from all the concrete examples of things with these qualities. Einstein said that there have been three stages in the development of the idea of God: a God based on fear; a God based on moral social factors; and the third is a cosmic spirit. Why have concepts of God changed over the centuries? On examination, it turns out that they are clearly based on the structure, sociology and cultural characteristics of the society giving birth to them. They are, therefore, human-made in humanity's own image. The reader will notice that I have written 'They are' in referring to concepts of God. For those of us for whom concepts of God may exist without any substantive base in reality, it follows that there is not one concept of God but many concepts, i.e. there are an unlimited number of forms in which (the concept of) God may exist. Monotheism is an authoritarian social imposition. There are as many Gods as there are people with ideas of God.

And it is here that I must mention a concept of God which is rooted in its time, which is referred to in Karen Armstrong's book, *The Bible. The Biography.* We can universalise this for our own time and circumstances.

It seems that, after the destruction of the temple in Judea in AD70, there was a Jewish religious revival, or perhaps it was a part of a general upsurge of which Jesus was another manifestation. It was the real beginning of the rabbinic tradition.

The scholars of that day were not, as we are, concerned with the original meaning of a given passage in the scriptures – they were looking for fresh interpretations. In other words, they were not treating the scriptures as if they were dead and ossified, but living and developing. Karen Armstrong explains that (as they saw it), because new events occur and things constantly change, even God has to continually study the Torah to keep up with its full significance. Moreover, whenever a Jew reads the scriptures, it has a different significance. Finally, and most profoundly, a text which cannot be reinterpreted must be dead. We must constantly revitalise texts in order to keep them alive. (*The Bible. The Biography,* pp.81-2).

There are two spiritual insights here, first to do with the idea of God and the second about the infinite inexhaustibility of any scriptural writing. The first sees the idea of God as self-referring because God has to return to his own creation (the Torah) and study that which he, himself, created, which must of necessity contain that of God within it. This may be generalised (by us) into the idea of God being self-referring in the most general sense and such a concept is strictly in correspondence with our own times. It is our own insight.

The link between this and the second insight lies in the fact that they saw God as having to study the Torah anew as change occurred in the universe and there would be developments of which it must take account. So God must study the Torah in the light of these new developments. God is thus self-referring and also ever-changing and developing through this study and through learning more and more about himself as a result of this study.

The second major insight - that of the inexhaustibility of the Torah (as they saw it) – has major implications for any religion basing itself on a book and also for any significant book, religious or otherwise, (e.g. the Bible, Koran or Shakespeare) and these implications are well-known and well-recognised in the case of secular writings. They have to be applied in the case of scriptures as well. It means that any scripture, if it is worthy of the name, must be infinitely reinterpretable by new readers and in the light of new happenings. Such scriptures, being supposedly inspired by an infinite God, must be of infinite depth. If they cannot be infinitely reinterpreted in this way, then they must be finite and, therefore, of little worth. In order that such scripture remains alive it must be reinterpretable, otherwise it will ossify and simply die.

That which is inspired by the infinitude of the universe must be seen as inexhaustible, and to fail to do this is to participate in the act of killing it. The early rabbis saw God re-reading the Torah and drew the right conclusions from this. They also understood that any Jew rereading the holy books should reinterpret them in the light of new happenings and that this reinterpretation was inexhaustible. Their thought was particular and limited, of necessity. We can, with hindsight, universalise and generalise this into the spiritually revolutionary idea of a constantly changing self-referring God and the inexhaustibility of all inspired writing.

Three different concepts of God have emerged in the course of this book. The first is that of an abstraction from abstractions from the concrete material world. Such a God is static. The second is the changing, historically determined, developmental one based on the concrete circumstances of the time. The final and most recent one is the self-referring God who changes intrinsically with a self-referring, but changing universe. The last might be said to embody the first two concepts and provide an idea of God that is both a (double) abstraction and is also self-referring. The model emerging from this would be of a self-referring God propelled by the instrumentality of self-referring conscious beings. The God-concept would be in process of self-realisation through the instrumentality of the universe itself. And the reader may rest assured that these insights, such as they are, have come to me as a nontheist. It now remains for me, as a nontheist, to wonder what such concepts imply for humanity's relationship to the cosmos.

However, the God-concept is only one of a limitless number of such concepts all of which are realising themselves in this way. Remember Meister Eckhart: 'The Godhead is as void as though it were not.' In other words, God is so empty of all attributes that it is as though he did not exist.

If the development of spirit results in non-experience of the transcendental it must be accepted as such. And since our ideas are part of the universe, it seems that we (as Subjects) may become aware that the 'other', the Object, which is nouminous, does not amount to a creator God. This awareness is as much an experience, a creative discovery as anything else and its occurrence as much a part of our self-transformation as any other.

Who Creates What?

In the course of writing, not only do one's ideas change but more and more questions are thrown up which demand, but may not produce, answers. How does mind transcend its perceived limits? At one moment it is a blank and yet, later, an answer may emerge unexpectedly. A mini-transformation has occurred, most probably via the neurones in the brain.

On achieving some sort of insight, it feels as if one has broken through the perceived limits. It is no wonder that Hegel thought of this as 'a finite mind infinitising' through cognition. And yet the solution to any problem is subject to objective constraints as in any perception. We cannot conceive of anything beyond the Suchness of our universe and the relationships between the elements which make it up. Thankfully, this still allows for limitless possibilities.

There is also the familiar problem that we are part of the universe we seek to understand and in order to relate to it we have to be separate from it and simultaneously connected. So full understanding is denied us as we may never be 'outside' that of which we are an integral part. So we are not gods. On the other hand, we constantly create something out of nothing in many different fields and this makes us 'gods' in this respect. The universe I see around me in all its vivid colour and shape has been 'created' by me within the terms of the objective constraints imposed by my perceptive mechanism.

A carpenter may have made the table I am looking at but I also have 'created' it as I see it, out of the Suchness which it truly is and would be were I not there. Not only that, but I exist by virtue of the innumerable interconnections I have with my milieu, including the table. And so, in a sense, it 'creates' me – at least it maintains me in my existence. Were I not connected to the elements in my milieu, which includes the table, I would implode and disappear! Even more does this apply to my social milieu. Had I been born in another culture I would think and behave quite differently.

My universe has created me just as the universe created Johann Sebastian Bach who was the channel for the composition of the Preludes and Fugues.

There is no climactic ending to this little book because I am still somewhere on my spiritual road and have no idea at what point. The question 'where'? obviously does not apply. There is no apparent end ...

Personal Finale

Although this section uses the word 'Finale' it has to be stressed that there are aspects of myself which do not feel that to be the case.

I would agree that, at the age of 85, there are many more years behind me than ahead. But that is only the case if we measure in conventional, socially determined years.

Provided my health remains reasonably good (of which there is absolutely no guarantee), I know that the years to come will provide unlimited fulfilment. That is because I am referring to my life's spiritual journey. I still have insights which give me intense pleasure. They may not be original in the sense that they may have never been said or written before by someone else. Nevertheless, many are original for me – I have insights that I have not heard before, read about or grasped previously. And this is in addition to the joys of music, friends, the natural world and other delights.

It has been highly satisfying to record my own spiritual journey, and many other people must have had (and be having) their own roads to self-discovery which should be revealed to all of us. The wonderful thing is that all our roads will be different. There is no prescription for the happiness of the spirit.

It feels *as if* there is infinite time ahead while my rational brain knows that there is not. For this I have to thank the relativity of infinity and the gift of not knowing one's future or exact date of death. It feels *as if* there is an infinite future with unlimited quality spiritual experience. And because I know this to be, in a sense, illusory I try not to waste this precious gift.

I feel rather like the Children of Israel may have felt when they recognised the differences between themselves and other tribes around them who were polytheistic and did not have the same moral code. They felt that they were a 'chosen' people. However, like them, I have chosen myself as have so many of my contemporaries who have the same experiences as I have.

Rereading this Finale, I question how anyone can be so happy in a world which is so deeply troubled, with so much poverty, suffering, injustice and misery, not to mention the threat of human extinction due to our plundering and misuse of resources?

I can only respond that, whilst I fully realise all this and do try, in however small a way, to contribute in the social and political sphere, I know that what one is able to do changes from one stage of life to another. I do appreciate that there is little I can do at the social and political level these days. I also know now, with the wisdom of age, that there was little I could do even when I was young, even though I thought I was helping to change the world for the better.

Many young people do not realise, and would not believe if told, that the best for them may be yet to come – theirs is the stage in life at which the business of life is carried on and this needs maximum concentration on achievement – for it is the intrinsic openness of consciousness which brings the spiritual rewards of old age. And the basic necessity for such openness is detachment, as the Buddhists know. And it is for many of us only in later life, having finished with the activities of family and work, that we can achieve the detachment needed for such spiritual growth.

The good news is that the prison door is open. We are free to walk out, to stand on our own feet and create our true spiritual selves through creating our very own (spiritual) models; that is, myths and metaphors. We do not have to look to some powerful 'grown-up' in the sky to tell us what to do and provide for us. We do not have to be bound by old rules, laws or habits. This might well make many people nervous (and has often done so) but we have to pluck up our courage and take heart.

There is a great responsibility on us to create a new and higher morality than has gone before; only our own deepest selves can provide the reference points and yardsticks for this. Such a difficult task can only be accomplished if we are 'in but not of this world' so that it is *as if* we were outside it and able to reflect upon it. And everybody will have their own special way of participating in this as we all have different life histories.

'Openness' to the cosmos is key. Faith is open. Belief is closed. That is why it is so hard to say what one believes in. The world is evanescent and constantly changing and the seeking mind and soul is challenged by this to keep up to speed. And we have to constantly be prepared for the unexpected. The really exciting thing is that the possibilities before us are limitless.

The problem with this in the spiritual sphere, especially with respect to the existence or not of God, is that freedom is very scary. However, if we were to imagine ourselves out in space, viewing our planet, we would see a sort of sphere rolling round and round in empty space, apparently entirely unsupported. And since the world is apparently entirely unafraid under these circumstances, neither should we be under ours.

Bibliography
(Books referred to in the text)

Armstrong, K. *The Bible. The Biography,* (Atlantic Books, 2008)

Armstrong, K. *The Case for God,* (The Bodley Head, 2009)

Boulton, D. *The Trouble with God: Building the Republic of Heaven,* (O Books, 2002)

Copernicus, N. *De Revolutionibus Orbium Coelestium,* (1543)

Davies, P. *God and the New Physics,* (Penguin Books, 1990)

Descartes, R. *La Géométrie,* (1637)

Eckhart von H. (Meister). *Selected Writings,* (Penguin Classics, 1994)

Einstein, A. and Infeld, L. *The Evolution of Physics,* Edited by C.P.Snow, (Cambridge University Press, 1938)

Ellis, G.F.R. *Before the Beginning: Cosmology Explained,* (Boyars/Bowerdean, 1993)

Euclid. *The Elements,* (Dover, 1956)

Gosse, E. *Father and Son,* (Scribner's sons, 1907)

Huxley, A. *The Perennial Philosophy,* (HarperCollins, 2004)

Laplace, P-S. *Traité de méchanique céleste,* (1799)

Marx, K. *Contribution to the Critique of Hegel's Philosophy of Right* in Christopher Hitchens, *The Portable Atheist,* (Da Capo Press, 2007)

Marx, K. and Engels, F. *The Communist Manifesto,* (1848)

Newton, I. *Philosophiae Naturalis Principia Mathematica,* (1687)

Newton, I. *Arithmetica Universalis,* (1707)

Quaker Faith and Practice, (Quaker Books, 2005)

Rotman, B. *Signifying Nothing. The Semiotics of Zero,* (St. Martin's Press, 1987)

Talbot, M. *The Holographic Universe,* (Harper Collins, 1996)

Wallis, J. *Algebra,* (1685)

Watts, A. *Myth and Ritual in Christianity,* (Thames and Hudson, 1954)

Wilber, K. (Ed.) *Quantum Questions,* (Shambhala Publications, 1984)